Endorsements

"Kim Boyce Koreiba and her husband Gary have been my good friends for many years, but I had no idea how much I would learn from their story and from this amazing book. If you have ever struggled with destructive forces that have brought pain and hurt into your life, you need to read this story. If you can't seem to forgive someone who has hurt you deeply, this book is for you. If you have wondered where God was when you have been brutally disconnected from everyone who "had your back," you need this book. And when those things that were your security have disappeared, I think you will find some answers in this treatise. This book will challenge you to re-evaluate your relationships. It will challenge you to recalculate those things in your life that seem important and redefine them in a new way...in the light of eternity. Reading the pages of this book today just might make the pages of your life read differently tomorrow. Remember this: a better future for you is not too far from here."

—GARY MCSPADDEN

Pastor, singer, songwriter

"Kim Boyce Koreiba is a dear friend who has the ability to communicate the very essence of her heart. In this book she's done that very thing in a beautiful and personal way. *Not Too Far from Here* is powerful and will encourage you to reach for high things by letting go!"

—CINDY CRUSE RATCLIFF

Senior worship leader for Joel Osteen Ministries

"I've known Kim for over thirty years, and I've always admired her music and ministry. I'm so proud of her for sharing in this book her experience of hurt to encourage others to move forward and find hope through the Word of God and His unfailing love."

—MARK LOWREY
Comedian, singer, songwriter "Mary, Did You Know?"

"I have such deep respect and admiration for Kim and Gary. They are a blessing. I love Kim's writing, but mostly, I love her heart, her honesty, her vulnerability and candor. *Not Too Far from Here* challenged me to pray, listen more, and not give up praying for certain issues. I am encouraged by Kim and her book."

—BARBARA IVEY BECK
Miss Florida 1971 and host of Welcome Home

"*Not Too Far from Here* spoke volumes to me as I read it. It's so powerfully charged with the Word! What an encouragement for women and men."

—JANICE BETZER
Director of Women's Ministry
Grace Community Assembly, Branson, Missouri

"Wow! Kim's most powerful work yet! Her advice and instructions are right on and hit the heart of the matter. *Not Too Far from Here* is rich with insight, meaning, and God's presence through it all. Her presentation isn't overwhelming, but still challenges us not to follow the path of common or worldly thought when it comes to dealing with hard things in our lives."

—LINDA LEE
Branson, Missouri

Moving
from
Hurt to
Hope

Not Too Far *from* Here

KIM BOYCE KOREIBA

BroadStreet
PUBLISHING

BroadStreet Publishing Group, LLC
Racine, Wisconsin, USA
www.broadstreetpublishing.com

Not Too Far *from* Here
Moving from Hurt to Hope

ISBN-13: 978-1-4245-4967-2 (print)
ISBN-13: 978-1-4245-5007-4 (e-book)

Unless otherwise noted, all Scripture is from the New King James Version®. Copyright © 1982 by Thomas Nelson. Used by permission. All rights reserved. Scripture marked NCV is from the New Century Version®. Copyright © 2005 by Thomas Nelson, Inc. Used by permission. All rights reserved. Scripture marked NIV is from THE HOLY BIBLE, NEW INTERNATIONAL VERSION®, NIV® Copyright © 1973, 1978, 1984, 2011 by Biblica, Inc.® Used by permission. All rights reserved worldwide. Scripture marked NLT is taken from the Holy Bible, New Living Translation, copyright © 1996, 2004, 2007 by Tyndale House Foundation. Used by permission of Tyndale House Publishers, Inc., Carol Stream, Illinois 60188. All rights reserved. Scripture marked KJV is from the King James Version, which is in the Public Domain. Scripture marked RSV is from the Revised Standard Version of the Bible, copyright © 1946, 1952, and 1971 the Division of Christian Education of the National Council of the Churches of Christ in the United States of America. Used by permission. All rights reserved. Scripture marked MSG is from The Message. Copyright © 1993, 1994, 1995, 1996, 2000, 2001, 2002. Used by permission of NavPress Publishing Group. Scripture marked CEV is from the Contemporary English Version®. Copyright © 1995 American Bible Society. All rights reserved.

Printed in China

15 16 17 18 19 20 5 4 3 2 1

Dedication

This book is dedicated to my husband, Gary Lee Koreiba, and our two wonderful sons, Gary Lee Koreiba II and Alexander Boyce Koreiba. We have walked this journey from hurt to hope together, and I thank God that you have been strong, godly men who have helped sustain me through this difficult season. I love you with all of my heart. Each of you is a gift for which I am eternally grateful.

Contents

Introduction

This book is for anyone who has been hurt. Hurt so badly that you couldn't breathe. Hurt so much that you weren't sure you could get out of bed. Hurt to the point that it was too hard to speak.

You go through the motions of another day, but when the day is over, you don't remember what you did for the past sixteen hours. You can't sleep. You don't eat. You attempt to present yourself as being okay for the sake of your kids or your spouse or your friends, but you're really not okay.

You question everything. *God, why is this happening? What did I do to deserve this? How will I recover from this? Am I ever going to feel normal again? Will I ever be happy again? Does God care about what I'm going through?*

I don't know what particular hurt you have gone through, but if you're like most people, you've been through many times of hurt in your life. We all have, but there are certain times and certain hurts and certain wounds that seem to cut deeper than others.

Research has shown that there are certain circumstances in life that cause a great deal of stress. Top stressors include the death of a spouse, divorce, the death of a close family member, a personal injury or illness, and loss of employment. Perhaps one of these events has caused you great pain. Maybe you've had several of these situations in your life, and you don't know how to deal with the hurt. Or you may have an entirely different list of hurts and disappointments that have caused you physical and/or emotional pain.

My husband, Gary, and I went through a very difficult time of hurt, disappointment, and discouragement that put a dark cloud over our normally sunny lives and dispositions. We have been through hard times in our twenty-plus years of marriage, but this circumstance was completely unexpected. We were blindsided, and the sense of betrayal that we experienced was something that we hope no one else ever has to go through.

I have a bachelor's degree in biblical counseling and a master's degree in Christian counseling. You would think my counseling degrees would have helped me know what to do during a time of great hurt, but my mind was blank. I knew only two things for certain. First, we had no idea what to do, and second, God did. He was not surprised, caught off guard, or scrambling to make sense of our situation. He was not in heaven recalculating the ramifications of this incident, nor was He instructing angels to implement Plan B. We were surprised, caught off guard, and scrambling, but God was not.

We have a great support system of godly family members and friends, pastors and mentors, and church family who have encouraged us throughout difficult times. These are the people we turned to within hours of our pain. As these spiritually mature people spoke to us, I knew their words were not just platitudes to ease our pain. They spoke words that were wise, inspired, and often prophetic. As words were spoken to us, I began to write them down. I would be talking with someone on the phone, and I would ask them to repeat what they had just spoken so I could write it down word for word. Gary would come back from running an errand and tell me that someone called him. He would tell me about the conversation, and I would grab my pen and paper and start writing.

A pattern emerged in the words that were spoken to us. Each conversation confirmed a previous one. With each word of wisdom, encouragement, and advice, we began to sense something that we had lost . . . hope.

We sought God's guidance and direction. We spent hours daily, individually and together, in prayer and study. We read the Scriptures seeking God. We read books that we had previously read and trusted to give us fresh insight. We went back to the drawing board on the basics of remaining faithful on our Christian journey.

My record of the words spoken to us turned into a journal of encouragement. I filled two three-ring binders with Scripture verses, quotes from books, written prayers, the words of trusted advisors, and my thoughts. That binder turned into this book.

I'm not writing because I want you to feel sorry for us or to wrap up this part of my life and get closure. There's no closure. We are still struggling. We are still seeking. We still have hard days, but we just have to keep moving forward encouraging each other.

We cannot become isolated, withdrawn, and filled with self-pity. We cannot get so bogged down that we wallow in a sinkhole of selfishness that believes that no one else has ever felt as we feel. Everyone has been hurt. Everyone has probably felt the way we feel. How selfish would it be to think no one has ever been through something much *more* painful?

So I'm writing this book for one reason. I'm writing because God "comforts us every time we have trouble, so when others have trouble, we can comfort them with the same comfort God gives us" (2 Corinthians 1:4 NCV).

I've been comforted by God's Word through a time of trouble, so my responsibility as a follower of Christ is to give of myself and comfort someone else. My prayer is that this book will bring you comfort, encouragement, direction, and hope.

Not Too Far *from* Here

Somebody's down to their last dime
Somebody's running out of time
Not too far from here
Somebody's got nowhere else to go
Somebody needs a little hope
Not too far from here
And I may not know their name
But I'm praying just the same
That You'll use me, Lord, to wipe away a tear
'Cause somebody's crying
Not too far from here

Somebody's troubled and confused
Somebody's got nothing left to lose
Not too far from here
Somebody's forgotten how to trust
Somebody's dying for love
Not too far from here
It may be a stranger's face
But I'm praying for Your grace
To move in me and take away the fear
'Cause somebody's hurting
Not too far from here

Help me, Lord, not to turn away from pain
Help me not to rest while those around me weep
Give me Your strength and compassion
When somebody finds the road of life too steep

Now I'm letting down my guard
And I'm opening my heart
Help me speak Your love to every needful ear
Jesus is waiting
Not too far from here [1]

Chapter 1

Good News and Bad News

January 7, 2013. Gary and I arrived at a production meeting for the very popular show in Branson, Missouri, that we had both sung in for thirteen and ten years respectively. During a three-minute meeting, we were told by our boss: "Well, good news and bad news. The bad news is tough. We're going to change directions in the show and not have you guys back next year . . . The good news is we're going to continue your paychecks, not indefinitely, but until you find work . . . You haven't done anything wrong . . . You surely have questions."

Our minds were blank. *No.* We couldn't think of any questions. We couldn't think period. I looked at Gary. The look of utter shock and disbelief on his face was heartbreaking.

When we moved to Branson, it was because we knew beyond a shadow of a doubt that God had called us there. We didn't particularly want to move. We didn't especially want, in effect, to retire from successful careers in contemporary Christian music. We made the move, however, because we had young sons whom we didn't want to raise on a tour bus. We moved because we didn't want to leave them at home while we toured. We moved because we wanted to be together as a family. And we moved because we prayed for God's will and direction. We asked all of our spiritually mature family members and friends to pray with us, and they all agreed this was a move we were supposed to make.

When we made the first trip to Branson for Gary to see and hear the group that had asked him to audition, we were unimpressed. The vocal group was mediocre. The comedian in the show, however, was fantastic, so the show had a good following.

As soon as the producer of the show heard Gary sing, he offered him the job on the spot. So in spite of the dingy theater that was the group's home, the cheesy country songs, and the Porter Wagoner outfits, Gary left his young family in Nashville a few weeks later and drove to Branson to start his new job.

I stayed behind with the boys to sell our house. Gary called me the first week he was in the show and said, "Don't plan on buying a house here. I don't think we're staying."

Gary may not have been impressed, but there was a buzz in town about the new guy. Within the small entertainment community, there was excitement in the air. The group sounded better than they had ever sounded.

Within weeks, there was a big meeting and everyone was told that the show was going to own their own theater. Actually, four investors would own the show and theater, but anyone who left their current job and came to the new show was promised all kinds of great incentives: profit sharing, health care, and other perks. It was going to be a family, a brotherhood. It was all for one and one for all, and the new show became the breakout hit of the decade in Branson.

Three years later, the comedian planned to leave, and Gary was asked if he thought I would join the show because the company could really use me. After turning the job down twice, I finally agreed to join the cast of the show when I was assured I could bring my five- and eight-year-old boys to work with me.

I estimate that in thirteen years, Gary performed in approximately 5,681 shows. In my ten years, I sang in approximately 3,435 shows. Gary walked up and down the flight of steps to his dressing room about forty thousand times. I don't even want to think about how many times I retouched my hair and makeup.

Thankfully, every paycheck we were ever paid during those thirteen years was good. Gary and I would talk about the positive aspects of our jobs: security, being home, raising our kids in a small town, etc. We were grateful for God's provision. Just like every other job in the world, however, there were problems.

In spite of thirteen years of unprecedented financial success, my husband never received one profit sharing check or company health care; yet he still believed he had been providentially called to his job. He was the driving vocal force and personality of the group. He felt the pressure to go out and lead the group. He wanted to make every audience feel as if they were seeing a fresh show every time they came. He didn't dwell on broken promises, and he counseled other employees to do the same.

When radio and TV interviews needed to be done, Gary

and I were sent. When someone was needed to represent the theater at local events, Gary and I were sent. We were told we could be there as long as we wanted, and that the class and elegance we brought could not be replaced. So we banked on those words and built our lives around the job, partly because Gary believed he had been called to minister to some of the other men at the theater.

Now here we were being told that we wouldn't be back. As we got up to leave, Gary spoke. He didn't yell or get angry. He didn't say, "How could you do this? We moved here from another state! I've put my heart and soul in this place! How could you fire *both of us* at the same time? What the heck?" Instead, he said, "I've had a ball." Then there was silence. It was obvious that the meeting was over, so we walked out. The last thing said to us was, "Sorry."

We walked to our car in stunned silence. It was as if I knew I was walking, but I didn't process any sensory information. As we drove out of the parking lot, Gary turned to me and said, "I'm sorry, babe."

"*You* don't have *anything* to be sorry for," I said.

The next day we had the difficult task of cleaning out our dressing rooms. Mine was easy to clean because I didn't have much personal stuff there. Gary's dressing room, however, was a different story. He had thirteen years' worth of memorabilia in his dressing room. His eight-by-five mirror was almost completely covered in family pictures. He had posters on the walls from my CCM album covers. He had my Number One plaques on the walls. For the entire time he had been there, he had filled the dressing room with things that meant something to him. And now he was cleaning it out.

Three members of the management staff came backstage to help. They cried as they helped us pack things into crates. As the last crate was being carried downstairs, I went back to Gary's dressing room. I found him cleaning the mirror. Through my tears, I grabbed some cleanser and started cleaning the sink. Gary went and got a vacuum cleaner, got down on his hands and knees, and with the hose vacuumed out every last bit of dust. I will never forget the image of my wonderful, godly, handsome, talented husband on his hands and knees vacuuming out his dressing room, straightening his costumes on the clothes rack, and lining up all of his cowboy boots. We both knew his replacement would be wearing those clothes the *next day* in a photo shoot.

We were the last to know we were being fired. Our replacements knew before we did. Some of the other staff members knew. We've been told that a businessman in the next town knew before we did.

Since we were fired, there have been some incredibly sleepless nights and tearful days. We felt for weeks as though we had been kicked in the gut. Some days we think we are doing okay, and then panic grips us. Fear starts to creep in. Logic demands the answer to the question *why?*

At this point, we don't know why this happened to us. And we especially don't know why it happened the *way* it happened. What about loyalty? What about brotherhood? Those were Gary's biggest questions. He felt called. He was dedicated. He was loyal. He *is* exceptionally talented. To be perfectly honest, the job was just a job to me. It was good money to sing. I got to live in my house, rather than live on the road. I got to be (almost) a full-time mom. My husband enjoyed me being there with him, so that's why I was there.

In ten years, I had had two disagreements with the producer over songs and wardrobe that I felt were inappropriate. One of those disagreements led to packing up my stuff and attempting to quit. My very loyal husband came into my dressing room, shut the door, and calmly said, "You can't do this and leave him in the lurch." So I stayed.

Then in one moment that took three minutes, our lives were turned upside down. My husband's sense of adequacy to provide for his family was temporarily taken away. The job he had put his heart and soul into was gone.

We had a vague promise that we would continue to be paid until we found other work, but this isn't about money. Money is important, but this is about my husband's faithfulness, loyalty, commitment, integrity, talent, and godliness being disrespected. It's about someone I love being treated unfairly. Sometimes watching someone you love suffer is far worse than enduring the suffering yourself.

Every human instinct in me wanted revenge. A few friends wanted to help with it. Several offered some creative ideas for enacting revenge, but those offers, while interesting, were turned down. I must admit, though, that some of the suggestions did make me laugh! God says revenge belongs to Him, and when I read the Old Testament, I realize that He is much better at it than I am. So I'll leave justice in His hands even though I may never see it.

In prayer, in seeking God's will and direction, and in attempting to not become angry and bitter, I was impressed with four things that I needed to do during this time: (1) Seek first the kingdom, (2) Love my enemies, (3) Fear not, and (4) Ask. I didn't believe I knew how to do those things very well, but I had a direction. I was on a mission. I had the ability to research. I had the desire to learn. And I had nothing else to do!

This book is organized around these four directives from the Lord. At the end of each chapter is a prayer and Scriptures that have encouraged and sustained me. I encourage you to take the time to read them, declare them out loud, meditate upon them, and receive the comfort, hope, and healing God has for you through them.

Gary and I are still learning what God has for us in this next phase of life and ministry. But we know the end result will be many great testimonies of what God has done. How do I *know*? "For I know the thoughts that I think toward you, says the LORD, thoughts of peace and not of evil, to give you a future and a hope" (Jeremiah 29:11). There is a promise I *know* will be kept. The next verse contains my responsibility: "Then you will call upon Me and go and pray to Me, and I will listen to you" (v. 12). Now, that's good news!

Part One

SEEK FIRST
THE KINGDOM

*The command to seek the kingdom of God and
his righteousness first enjoins us to treat this subject
as of absolute and supreme importance.
This must be the great business of our lives.*
—*Charles Finney*

t is not circumstance or coincidence that the first directive I
felt given to me in the journey of moving from hurt to hope
is *Seek First the Kingdom*. Jesus gave specific instructions when
He said, "Therefore do not worry, saying, 'What shall we eat?'
or 'What shall we drink?' or 'What shall we wear?' For after all
these things the Gentiles seek. For your heavenly Father knows
that you need all these things. But seek first the kingdom of
God and His righteousness, and all these things shall be added
to you. Therefore do not worry about tomorrow, for tomorrow

will worry about its own things. Sufficient for the day is its own trouble" (Matthew 6:31–34). Amen! Every day does have enough trouble of its own.

The Message version of this passage of Scripture is enlightening. It reads: "People who don't know God and the way he works fuss over these things, but you know both God and how he works. Steep your life in God-reality, God-initiative, God-provisions. Don't worry about missing out. You'll find all your everyday human concerns will be met."

Steeping our lives in what *The Message* calls "God-reality, God-initiative, and God-provisions" helps us see our circumstances from God's perspective. We must readjust our perspective to fit God's perspective because we do not see or know what God sees and knows. He has an eternal perspective; we have a temporary perspective. He is interested in eternal life, while we, many times, become overwhelmed with earthly life. We worry. We get discouraged. We become depressed. We become self-absorbed. We cannot see past the hurt and pain that we are feeling today.

Seeking first the kingdom will help us become attentive to the things that really matter. It's what the old-timers used to call being "heavenly-minded." Being heavenly-minded can give you a more balanced perspective of today's problem. Kenneth Boa says that the heavenly-minded person can "treasure the passing opportunities of this life and become more alive to the present moment. Rather than being overwhelmed with the problems of life, they understand that these too will pass and that 'the sufferings of this present time are not worthy to be compared with the glory that is to be revealed to us' (Romans 8:18). Instead of taking things for granted, they learn to savor blessings and joys that are otherwise overlooked."[2]

So *how* do we seek first the kingdom? By choosing to focus on things that last for eternity, rather than the "stuff" that will consume us if we allow it to. We cannot serve two masters (Matthew 6:24), so we need to choose wisely. As Bob Dylan sang many years ago, "You gotta serve somebody." I pray that you will choose to serve God and seek first the kingdom as you journey from hurt to hope. May these priorities, as Finney said, become "the great business of our lives."

Jesus tells us to set our hearts on the kingdom.
Setting our hearts on something involves not only our
serious aspiration but also strong determination.
A spiritual life requires human effort. The forces that
keep pulling us back into a worry-filled life are far
from easy to overcome.
—*Henri Nouwen*

Chapter 2

Trust God

Trust and obey
For there's no other way
To be happy in Jesus
Than to trust and obey [3]

Four days before Gary and I were fired, I wrote a blog for my website that said:

> I love the beginning of a new year! It feels like a fresh start. I don't like to make New Year's resolutions because they usually don't last very long. I do, however, like to spend time seeking direction for the coming year. For 2013, I believe that the direction I've been given is this: God is God, and I am not!

> This phrase comes from the book *Counseling: How to Counsel Biblically* by John MacArthur, and as so often happens, God speaks to me when I don't know that I'm even listening.

"God alone is eternal; He knows the end from the beginning, and thus He is able to comprehend exactly how all things will in fact 'work together for good,' no matter how distressing some of those things might seem to us . . . Therefore, God deserves to be honored, worshiped, trusted, feared, and loved as God. Our responsibility and privilege is to glorify Him: to enhance His reputation in the minds of rational creatures and to live our lives and order our days so that all who encounter us will have a higher regard for God than they might have had had they never encountered us!

But our besetting temptation is to glorify self: to live life as if we were the center of the universe, as if the enhancement of our reputation were a meritorious pursuit, and as if our contentment were the greatest good of the cosmos. That is why every believer must continually be confronted with the demand that God be honored as God."[4]

To live by the words "God is God and I am not" will require an understanding of the words of Jesus in John 12:25, "He who loves his life loses it; and he who hates his life in this world shall keep it for eternal life." It will require self-denial and self-sacrifice to understand that I can't make things happen, I'm not in control, and I don't run the show of my own life. It will mean accepting things that I would normally balk at. It will mean keeping my mouth shut when I would rather say what I think.

> Crud! Do I really want to have these words as my directive for 2013? No, I probably don't, but I believe that I'm supposed to, so here goes. This could be an interesting year!

God knew what would happen four days after I wrote the blog. He knew that I would need to be reminded that He is God. A.W. Tozer wrote, "What comes into our minds when we think about God is the most important thing about us."[5] So what comes into my mind when I think about God? I believe that God is all-powerful, all-knowing, good, just, and unchanging. God is holy, merciful, loving, and wise. God is faithful.

In a time of hurt and despair, we need to know that God is faithful. We need to know beyond the shadow of a doubt that He can be trusted. Someone, something, or some circumstance has hurt us badly, and our only hope lies in believing that God will do what He said in His Word that He would do. We must believe that He is trustworthy and that we have hope to live life abundantly (John 10:10), and through Jesus Christ, we have a hope of glory, an eternity in heaven (Colossians 1:5).

God is trustworthy. He loves us so much that He "demonstrates His

> The Bible teaches that we are only in a position to experience God's power and strength when we understand how weak we are, because that is when we abandon hope in our own resources and rely entirely on God. Our confidence should never be in our own strength, but in His.
>
> —JOHN MACARTHUR[6]

own love toward us, in that while we were still sinners, Christ died for us" (Romans 5:8). Christ is the Son of God. I have two sons. I don't love anyone on this earth enough to sacrifice one of my sons for them. I'm sorry, but that's the truth. If you are a parent, would you? But that is exactly what God did. Even though He knew that some of those He loved would reject Him, He made the sacrifice. He gave His perfect, sinless Son for you and me. I cannot comprehend the love He has for us, but I can be amazed by it and thankful for it. If He loves me that much, then I believe I can trust Him.

There are times when we have no option but to trust God. We are powerless in our own strength to help ourselves. These are the times when a believer in God's trustworthiness has to rely on God's Word to be true. We have to rely on the fact that He said, "My grace is enough for you. When you are weak, my power is made perfect in you" (2 Corinthians 12:9 NCV). Paul went on to say: "For this reason I am happy when I have weaknesses, insults, hard times, sufferings, and all kinds of troubles for Christ. Because when I am weak, then I am truly strong" (2 Corinthians 12:10 NCV).

This would be a good time to write a list of the times in your life when God has proven Himself to be trustworthy. Some small thing that happened may have seemed trivial at the time, but you may look back on it later and realize it was a divinely orchestrated event. I write things down because I tend to forget them quickly. If you are like me, the realization of God's faithfulness may come, and then two minutes later, you can't remember what you realized. That is why writing is important. I started writing things down in a journal consistently about twelve years ago, and I find it encouraging to reread the entries. It is sad how little I remember without prompting from the journals. There are numerous examples in the Old Testament where the Israelites built an altar or stacked stones as a reminder of something God had done. They used these visuals so they would not forget the ways God had shown His trustworthiness and faithfulness on their behalf. Writing in a journal is my way of doing the same. My journals take up much less space than a yard full of stacked stones!

There's always another giant.

—TIM BROOKS, Pastor
Christian Ministries Church,
Hot Springs, Arkansas

When I need encouragement, I turn to the stories, testimonies, and writings of the great heroes of the Christian faith. One of my heroes is Billy Graham. There is a sidebar in my Bible that quotes one of his books. It reads, "Christ living in us will enable us to live above our circumstances, however painful they are . . . You wonder how much more you can stand. But don't despair! God's grace is sufficient for you and will enable you to rise above your trials. Let this be your confidence: 'Can anything separate us from the love Christ has for us? Can troubles or problems or sufferings or hunger or nakedness or danger or violent death? . . . But in all these things we are completely victorious through God who showed his love for us'" (Romans 8:35–37).[7]

A Diary of Private Prayer by John Baillie has a prayer that gave me specific direction to follow every day while I was walking through this time of discouragement and disappointment. I wrote down the points in the prayer, and I read through them daily in order to have a list of things to do to move forward in a positive spiritual direction:

1. Get up early to seek God.
2. Praise God for His loving kindness and righteous judgments.
3. Take heed according to His Word.
4. Be taught by the Word and wait.
5. Speak carefully.
6. Ask God to order my steps.
7. Walk uprightly.
8. Make my words and thoughts acceptable to God.[8]

I believe this prayer spoke God's will to me for this difficult time. Accomplishing the things on the list will keep me busy. Just accomplishing number five will be a big challenge! I urge you to use this list to help in your situation too. Each item is a biblical principle that will bring positive change to your heart, attitude, life, and relationship with God Almighty.

When you have a need, you can find fulfillment. When life on this earth seems unbearable, you have the hope of eternity free from sorrow and pain. When you are hurting, you are promised comfort. "Heavens and earth, be happy. Mountains, shout with joy, because the LORD comforts his people and will have pity on those who suffer" (Isaiah 49:13 NCV). In the Beatitudes, Jesus said, "Those people who know they have great spiritual needs are happy, because the kingdom of heaven belongs to them. Those who are sad now are happy, because God will comfort them. Those who are humble are happy, because the earth will belong to them. Those who want to do right more than anything else are happy, because God will fully satisfy them. Those who show mercy to others are happy, because God will show mercy to them. Those who are pure in their thinking are happy, because they will be with God. Those who work to bring peace are happy, because God will call them his children. Those who are treated badly for doing good are happy, because the kingdom of heaven belongs to them" (Matthew 5:3–10 NCV).

I read somewhere that life is a test and a trust. It's a test because decisions that we make during our time on this earth determine our eternal destiny. It's a trust because God entrusted mankind with a free will to believe (or disbelieve) in the reliability, truth, ability, and strength of His character. God is omnipotent, all-powerful. His Word says that "all things work together for good to those who love God, to those who are the called according to His purpose" (Romans 8:28). So do I believe that God is in control and that He is working all things together for my good?

> To keep going in this world, doing one's duty in spite of the uncertainties and ambiguities of life with the hope that God, somehow, somewhere, will make things balance—this is the last summary of this marvelous man's thoughts.
>
> —JAMES EFIRD, in reference to the book of Ecclesiastes[9]

Can I trust that He loves me even though the circumstances in my life appear to be anything but good? Can I hold on a little longer to see what He is going to do?

Prayer

God, You are God, and I am not. I trust in You. I trust that You are working all things together for my good because I am called according to Your purpose. I believe that You love me and have a plan for my life that is greater than I could imagine. I can't dream a dream too big for You to be able to accomplish, but I admit my weakness to accomplish anything in my own power without Your help. I abandon hope in my resources, talent, intelligence, and abilities. I am broken, and I have no confidence in my own strength. So now I am in a position to experience *Your* power and strength. I rely completely upon You as my source, resource, and strength. My confidence is in You! May I depend on You to bring victory in my circumstance. Give me peace because I trust in You. Speak to me, and may I be aware of and receptive to Your voice. Lead me in the way that You would have me to go. Comfort me when I am in distress. I give You control of my life, and ask that Your will would be accomplished in it. In the name of Jesus Christ I pray.

The Promises of God

I am offering you life or death, blessings or curses. Now, choose life! Then you and your children may live. To choose life is to love the Lord your God, obey him, and stay close to him. He is your life, and he will let you live many years in the land, the land he promised to give your ancestors Abraham, Isaac, and Jacob.

Deuteronomy 30:19–20 NCV

You will keep him in perfect peace, whose mind is stayed on You, because he trusts in You.

Isaiah 26:3

We are troubled on every side, yet not distressed; we are perplexed, but not in despair; persecuted, but not forsaken; cast down, but not destroyed.

2 Corinthians 4:8–9 KJV

At that time people will say, "Our God is doing this! We have waited for him, and he has come to save us. This is the Lord. We waited for him."

Isaiah 25:9 NCV

"For I know the plans I have for you," declares the Lord, "plans to prosper you and not to harm you, plans to give you hope and a future. Then you will call on me and come and pray to me, and I will listen to you. You will seek me and find me when you seek me with all your heart."

Jeremiah 29:11–13 NIV

The LORD always keeps his promises; he is gracious in all he does. The LORD helps the fallen and lifts those bent beneath their loads. The eyes of all look to you in hope; you give them food as they need it.

Psalm 145:13–15 NLT

The LORD is close to everyone who prays to him, to all who truly pray to him. He gives those who respect him what they want. He listens when they cry, and he saves them.

Psalm 145:18–19 NCV

Chapter 3

Obey God

When I hear Your voice and follow You, my life is full.
When I get off the path You have for me, my life is empty.
—Stormie Omartian[10]

•••

True Christians are people who acknowledge
and live under the word of God.
—J.I. Packer[11]

When our boys were very young, we taught them the Ten Commandments. We didn't teach them the King James Version of the commandments. The archaic language would have meant nothing to small boys. We taught them the paraphrased version from *The Hosanna Bible*, a children's Bible that Gary's cousin, Angela Abraham, had written.

Recently, we taught the high school Sunday school class at our church, and to teach the Ten Commandments, we used the same paraphrased version that we had taught our boys. They read:

1. I am the only, one true God. Love and worship Me.
2. Do not worship or serve any other other god.
3. Do not curse or swear using God's name.
4. Rest on the Sabbath Day; keep it holy.
5. Honor your father and your mother.
6. Do not kill people.
7. Husbands and wives, be faithful to each other.
8. Do not steal.
9. Do not lie.
10. Do not wish for things that belong to someone else.

If you prefer a more traditional list of the Ten Commandments, you can find them in Exodus 20. For me, however, this one works just fine. The commandments are straightforward, easy to understand, make the point concisely, and are easy to remember.

The Ten Commandments are the first commandments God gave to Israel when they left Egypt and officially became a nation, and they are the starting point in a life of obedience for the Christian today. There are many other commands, including what Jesus called "The Greatest Commandment" (which we will examine in the next chapter), but the Ten Commandments are foundational to living a life of obedience.

An honest self-examination of obedience and disobedience based upon these commandments will provide the starting point for "putting off the old man" and "putting on the new man" as Ephesians 4:22–24 teaches. Biblical counseling calls this the put-off/put-on principle: "The key fact here is that Paul does not only say 'put off' the old man (i.e., the old lifestyle), but also says 'put on' the new man (i.e., the Christian lifestyle). Change is a two-factored process. These two factors always must be present in order to effect genuine change. Putting off will not be permanent without putting on. Putting on is hypocritical as well as temporary, unless it is accompanied by putting off."[12]

There is an enlightening passage of Scripture that addresses repentance. In Judges 10:15 (NCV), the Israelites found themselves in a situation that forced them to examine their sin. They said, "We have sinned. Do to us whatever you want, but please save us today!" The next verse (v. 16) tells what they did to prove their sincerity in repenting: "Then the Israelites threw away the foreign gods among them, and they worshiped the LORD again. So he felt sorry for them when he saw their suffering."

So the Israelites:

1. Repented ("We have sinned").
2. Accepted the consequences ("Do to us whatever you want").
3. Asked for help ("Please save us today").
4. Stopped the sin ("The Israelites threw away the foreign gods").
5. Worshiped God ("And worshiped the LORD").

And then what happened? "He felt sorry for them when he saw their suffering." God had compassion on them. God is unchanging, so the good news for us is that He still feels sorry for us when He sees our suffering!

If the politically incorrect term *sin*—disobedience to God's commands—has caused you to be in the undesirable place you are in today, then repentance and a 180-degree turn toward obedience is necessary to fixing the problem and starting the healing process. To quote Dr. Phil when he is counseling someone who is obviously (at least partially) responsible for the problem that they find themselves in, "How's that workin' for ya?"

From a Christian counseling perspective, I suggest that you examine your own responsibility in your situation and circumstances; and if you know you are partially (or wholly) at fault, and you do not know how to change your habits and/or thought patterns, seek Christian counseling.

Often, it is necessary to ask a friend, family member, trusted advisor, or professional counselor for insight on personal problems and situations. Several times throughout the course of the recent journey that Gary and I have walked through, we have consulted with our pastor. I've studied counseling enough to know that my own perceptions of our circumstances can be skewed because of feelings and emotions, so we have sought outside counsel. It's not an admission of weakness or mental instability to seek counsel. It is wise. Proverbs 15:22 says, "Without counsel, plans go awry, but in the multitude of counselors they are established." Choose your counselors wisely. They should be those whose lives you admire. People who you know to have excellent reputations and who have lived lives obedient to Christ. Don't search for a perfect counselor/advisor because you won't find one, but be diligent in your search for wisdom, counsel, and advice from several people whom you trust.

Being obedient to God's commands is not easy. It is not the norm in society today. It is often not our instinctive reaction to a situation, but we can be assured that we will move from hurt to hope much faster if we obey God, rather than obeying man (Acts 5:29). This is because the results of an obedient life are exactly what we desperately need when we are struggling.

Some of the results of an obedient life are:

Friendship with God—"You are My friends if you do whatever I command you" (John 15:14). "He who has My commandments and keeps them, it is he who loves Me. And he who loves Me will be loved by My Father, and I will love him and manifest Myself to him" (John 14:21).

Joy—"These things I have spoken to you, that My joy may remain in you, and that your joy may be full" (John 15:11).

Provision—"And God gives us what we ask for because we obey God's commands and do what pleases him" (1 John 3:22 NCV).

Mercy—"If you hide your sins, you will not succeed. If you confess and reject them, you will receive mercy" (Proverbs 28:13 NCV). "Not by works of righteousness which we have done, but according to His mercy He saved us, through the washing of regeneration and renewing of the Holy Spirit" (Titus 3:5).

God's goodness—"Oh, how great is Your goodness, which You have laid up for those who fear You, which You have prepared for those who trust in You in the presence of the sons of men" (Psalm 31:19).

Justice—"Say to people who are frightened, 'Be strong. Don't be afraid. Look, your God will come, and he will punish your enemies. He will make them pay for the wrongs they did, but he will save you'" (Isaiah: 35:4 NCV).

> Provision follows
> obedience.
>
> —DAN BETZER, Pastor
> First Assembly of God,
> Fort Myers, Florida

Blessing—"But he who looks into the perfect law of liberty and continues in it, and is not a forgetful hearer but a doer of the work, this one will be blessed in what he does" (James 1:25).

Safety—"In peace I will lie down and sleep, for you alone, O LORD, will keep me safe" (Psalm 4:8 NLT). "You, LORD, will keep the needy safe and will protect us forever from the wicked" (Psalm 12:7 NIV).

Reap the rewards of these benefits and blessings of obedience as you journey from hurt to hope.

Prayer

God, Please let me hear Your voice and follow You. I repent, and turn from all my transgressions, so that iniquity will not be my ruin. Cast away from me all the transgressions which I have committed, and give me a new heart and a new spirit (Ezekiel 18:30–31).

I want to obey You and follow your command-ments. Please "let the words of my mouth and the meditation of my heart be acceptable in Your sight, O LORD, my strength and my Redeemer" (Psalm 19:14).

I want to put off the old me with my ways of think-ing, doing, and being. Help me to put on Your ways. I want to think Your thoughts, do all that I do as though I'm doing it for You, and become the person You created me to be. And I can't do any of these things without Your guidance and strength, so guide and strengthen me, Lord, for this journey. I pray, God, that I always obey Your laws and commands. Give me the ability to do so. I don't want to suffer the consequences of disobedience. May Your Holy Spirit rest on me and give me wisdom, understand-ing, and power to live a life obedient to Your Word and commands. In Your mighty name I pray.

The Promises of God

But Samuel answered, "What pleases the LORD more: burnt offerings and sacrifices or obedience to his voice? It is better to obey than to sacrifice. It is better to listen to God than to offer the fat of sheep. Disobedience is as bad as the sin of sorcery. Pride is as bad as the sin of worship-ing idols. You have rejected the LORD's command. Now he rejects you as king."

1 Samuel 15:22–23 NCV

If you had obeyed me, you would have had peace like a full-flowing river. Good things would have flowed to you like the waves of the sea.

Isaiah 48:18 NCV

This is what I told them: "Obey me, and I will be your God, and you will be my people. Do everything as I say, and all will be well!"

Jeremiah 7:23 NLT

Then Peter and the other apostles answered and said, We ought to obey God rather than men.

Acts 5:29 KJV

"Wash yourselves and make yourselves clean. Stop doing the evil things I see you do. Stop doing wrong. Learn to do good. Seek justice. Punish those who hurt others. Help the orphans. Stand up for the rights of the widows." The LORD says, "Come, let us talk about these things. Though your sins are like scarlet, they can be as white as snow. Though your sins are deep red, they can be white like wool. If you become willing and obey me, you will eat good crops from the land. But if you refuse to obey and if you turn against me, you will be destroyed by your enemies' swords." The LORD himself said these things.

Isaiah 1:16–20 NCV

Now by this we know that we know Him, if we keep His commandments. He who says, "I know Him," and does not keep His commandments, is a liar, and the truth is not in him. But whoever keeps His word, truly the love of God is perfected in him. By this we know that we are in

Him. He who says he abides in Him ought himself also to walk just as He walked.

1 John 2:3–6

Obey his laws and commands that I am giving you today so that things will go well for you and your children. Then you will live a long time in the land that the LORD your God is giving to you forever.

Deuteronomy 4:40 NCV

Today I am letting you choose a blessing or a curse. You will be blessed if you obey the commands of the LORD your God that I am giving you today. But you will be cursed if you disobey the commands of the LORD your God. So do not disobey the commands I am giving you today, and do not worship other gods you do not know.

Deuteronomy 11:26–28 NCV

Chapter 4

✥

Love God

Then one of the scribes came, and having heard them rea-
soning together, perceiving that He had answered them well,
asked Him, "Which is the first commandment of all?" Jesus
answered him, "The first of all the commandments is: 'Hear,
O Israel, the LORD our God, the LORD is one. And you shall
love the LORD your God with all your heart, with all your
soul, with all your mind, and with all your strength.' This is
the first commandment. And the second, like it, is this: 'You
shall love your neighbor as yourself.' There is no other com-
mandment greater than these."

—Mark 12:28–31

To love God you must first *know* Him. You must understand
what He has done. This causes love for Him. "We love Him,
because He first loved us" (1 John 4:19 KJV). "I am graven on the
palms of his hands. I am never out of his mind. All of my knowledge of him depends on his sustained initiative in knowing me.

I know him because he first knew me, and continues to know me. He knows me as a friend, one who loves me; and there is no moment when his eye is off me, or his attention distracted from me, and no moment, therefore, when his care falters."[13] No matter what we have done, or what we have been through, or how badly we have been hurt, God's care never stops.

The foremost way that we come to know God and love God is through His Word. It is through His Word that we learn His attributes or who He is. In Scripture, He has spoken through the prophets and apostles, and has revealed Himself through His Son. Through Scripture, we also learn what He does. Here is a sampling of verses that teach why God's Word is so important to His children:

> Let all my reading so refresh my mind that I may the more eagerly seek after whatsoever things are pure and fair and true.
>
> —JOHN BAILLIE[21]

"All Scripture is given by inspiration of God, and is profitable for doctrine, for reproof, for correction, for instruction in righteousness, that the man of God may be complete, thoroughly equipped for every good work" (2 Timothy 3:16–17).

"For the word of God is living and powerful, and sharper than any two-edged sword, piercing even to the division of soul and spirit, and of joints and marrow, and is a discerner of the thoughts and intents of the heart" (Hebrews 4:12).

"So shall My word be that goes forth from My mouth; it shall not return to Me void, but it shall accomplish what I please, and it shall prosper in the thing for which I sent it" (Isaiah 55:11).

"The law of the Lord is perfect, converting the soul; the testimony of the Lord is sure, making wise the simple; the statutes of the Lord are right, rejoicing the heart; the commandment of the Lord is pure, enlightening the eyes; the fear of the Lord is clean, enduring forever; the judgments of the Lord are true and righteous altogether. More to be desired are they than gold, yea, than much fine gold; sweeter also than honey and the honeycomb. Moreover by them Your servant is warned, and in keeping them there is great reward" (Psalm 19:7–11).

When we obey God's commands, we express our love for Him. "Christian love has God for its primary object, and expresses itself first of all in implicit obedience to His commandments (John 14:15, 21,23; 15:10; 2 John 6). Self-will, that is self-pleasing, is the negation of love to God."[14]

In Mark 12:28–31, Jesus told the scribe that we must love God in four distinct areas of our human capacities:

Heart—When Jesus quotes the Scriptures and reiterates that we must love God with our hearts, He is affirming the Jewish understanding that the heart includes a person's emotions, reason, and will.[15] Therefore, loving God with your heart is not merely affection toward the Creator, but it is *feeling* lovingly toward God, *thinking* and discussing the attributes of God, and *determining* to submit human desires to His commands.

Soul—In modern thought, the soul is often associated with the psyche. In ancient Hebrew thought, the soul is "the direct aftermath of God breathing (blowing) His gift of life into a person, making them an ensouled being."[16] It is our spirit; the part of us that experiences eternal life after death. "Then the dust will return to the earth as it was, and the spirit will return to God who gave it" (Ecclesiastes 12:7). Loving God with our soul is loving Him completely from the core of our being. Loving Him from the part of ourselves that will live forever. Decisions made from loving God with my soul will be vastly different from decisions made based upon what I think is best for me now. Wow! Ponder that thought for a moment.

Mind—"On being asked as to which was the most important of all commandments, Jesus replied by quoting the *Shema* (Deuteronomy 6:4–5) which pious Jews recited daily, but He added, as did the lawyer in Luke 10:27, to what was stated in the Old Testament that God was to be loved with the *mind* as well as with the other human faculties."[17] The mind is intellectual, reasonable, logical, and God wants us to love Him by thinking intellectually, reasonably, and logically about Him. Human intellect does not frighten God. He is not concerned that we will outsmart Him. Jesus, by adding the word *mind* to the list, was encouraging thoughtful, reasoned thinking about God. He knew that the process would bring about change. "And do not be conformed to this world, but be transformed by the renewing of your mind, that you may prove what is that good and acceptable and perfect will of God" (Romans 12:2).

Strength—In the New Testament, strength is defined as ability, power, and might.[18] Loving God with our strength, therefore, is our determination to use our gifts, talents, time, and efforts to love God. It is a daily decision, a determined effort, to love God by the way that we choose to live. It is doing what God commands us to do when we don't feel like doing it. It is believing His Word when our emotions are telling us something different. It is digging in your heels and deciding to be "a worker who is not ashamed and who uses the true teaching in the right way" (2 Timothy 2:15 NCV). It is choosing to move from hurt to hope because our hope is in Him.

What if you do all you can to love God and you still have problems (which you will)? What if the circumstances don't appear to be changing, and you are ready to give up? Then it's time to learn a lesson from a man who endured great pain and suffering.

> For we are so preciously loved by God that we cannot even comprehend it. No created being can ever know how much and how sweetly and how tenderly God loves them.
>
> —JULIAN OF NORWICH

Job was an extremely wealthy man. He was blessed with a huge fortune, a large family, servants, and possessions. In one day, he lost *everything* (except, strangely, his nagging wife!). After Job has been sitting on an ash heap, scraping his sores, and listening to his wife and so-called friends' bad advice for about thirty-seven chapters in the Bible, God speaks and asks, "Where were you when I laid the foundations of the earth?" (Job 38:4). In other words, "I am God and you are not, so think about Me and get some perspective here." Perhaps Job remembered what he had said earlier to his friends: "Though He slay me, yet will I trust Him" (Job 13:15).

Job was eventually rewarded for his faithfulness by the restoration of his fortune and family. So what did he learn? "The lesson Job learned is that relationship with God, real religion, can sustain one no matter what the external situations may be."[19] *No matter what the external situations may be.* The "moral" of the story of Job is that a relationship with God—loving God—can get you through anything. But here's the kicker: Job never knew why he was so severely tested!

> There is only one way to love God: to take not a single step without him, and to follow with a brave heart wherever he leads.
> —FRANÇOIS FÉNELON[20]

"Why?" This one question can be the source of much grief. You and I want to know *why.* We want a reason. But there are some things that we will never know why. "You have been grieved by various trials, that the genuineness of your faith, being much more precious than gold that perishes, though it is tested by fire, may be found to praise, honor, and glory at the revelation of Jesus Christ" (1 Peter 1:6–7).

If following Jesus Christ meant an immediate solution to every problem in life, everyone would follow Him. But they would follow because of the benefits that they wanted to receive. Jesus wants followers who follow because they *love Him*, not because they love what they think He can do for them. He wants true disciples who will learn to live His way, in spite of problems, heartache, and sorrow. He wants to help get you through these things, not prevent you from having them.

He wants you to be tested so your faith in Him is proven genuine. We are required to pass the test.

The finite, created mind of man can never truly comprehend the majesty of the infinite, uncreated God. We can only "see through a glass, darkly" (1 Corinthians 13:12 KJV), but we are promised that if we seek Him wholeheartedly, we will find Him (Jeremiah 29:13). We find that He loved us so much that He gave Himself for us, and this thought should cause us to love God with all of our heart, mind, soul, and strength.

Prayer

God, I want to love You with all of my heart, soul, mind, and strength. And I want to love my neighbor as myself. Teach me how to do these things. They are completely the opposite of what my flesh cries out to do, so I will need Your Holy Spirit to empower me. I ask that You give me a desire to study Your Word. May the words that You have spoken cause me to love You and come to truly know You. Holy Spirit, I ask that You would inspire me to seek God. Teach me what I need to know to get through what I need to get through.

The Promises of God

For God so loved the world, that he gave his only begotten Son, that whosoever believeth in him should not perish, but have everlasting life.

John 3:16 KJV

For to be carnally minded is death; but to be spiritually minded is life and peace.

Romans 8:6 KJV

You will seek me and find me when you seek me with all your heart.

Jeremiah 29:13 NIV

Give your worries to the LORD, and he will take care of you. He will never let good people down.

Psalm 55:22 NCV

I love them that love me; and those that seek me early shall find me.

Proverbs 8:17 KJV

Every word of God is pure; he is a shield unto them that put their trust in him.

Proverbs 30:5 KJV

Yet in all these things we are more than conquerors through Him who loved us. For I am persuaded that neither death not life, nor angels nor principalities nor powers, nor things present nor things to come, nor height nor depth, nor any other created thing, shall be able to separate us from the love of God which is in Christ Jesus our Lord.

Romans 8:37–39

Part Two

LOVE YOUR ENEMIES

*True forgiveness is the hardest thing
in the universe.*
—David Augsburger

The greatest spiritual struggle that I have ever encountered is to forgive the man who broke my husband's heart. (After I wrote these words, I asked Gary to read them because I did not want the words "broke my husband's heart" to seem melodramatic or less than manly. I asked if they accurately described the emotion, and his words stabbed my heart. He said, "Well, I can tell you that I've *never* been betrayed like that before . . . not by someone who put his arm around me and called me his brother.") Everything within me wanted to hate that man. Even today, as I am writing, I am carefully choosing my words and focusing on the process that I have used in attempting to move on. But to be perfectly honest, my blood pressure is rising, and a familiar tightness in my chest is occurring just thinking about describing the situation. Sometimes it just happens . . . so the journey from hurt to hope continues.

As a Christian, I know that I am not allowed to hate him. I know that the commandments of God state that He would enact the vengeance that He deemed to be just. But all it takes is one flash of the memory of my husband's face while we were being fired, and I can be on the warpath again.

I was working on my master's degree in Christian counseling when we were fired. I immediately stopped working on it because I didn't want to keep studying how to counsel others when I could barely counsel myself. It took eight months for me to feel I was ready to start my studies again. I called a professor whose classes I had taken and asked her for academic advice on getting back into my program. As we discussed my plans, I told her the name of the next course that was listed on my course schedule.

She said, "I'm sorry, Kim, but that course is no longer being offered, so you will need to choose a new course that will fulfill the academic requirements of your program."

"Okay. What do you suggest?" I asked.

"I recommend that all of my counseling students take a very valuable course called Interpersonal Forgiveness," she said.

What, God? This must be one of those times when You are sitting up in heaven with a smirk on Your face because You knew what was coming! Interpersonal Forgiveness? Seriously? Really, God, You know that it has taken me eight months to feel that I can think straight again, and now the first course I'm going to take is Interpersonal Forgiveness? Yet even in my questioning, I knew the phone call to my professor was a divine appointment to get me back on the road to wholeness. So I signed up for the course, and I learned most of what I will write in this section. My prayer is that these all-important principles will help you.

Chapter 5

Forgive

Forgiveness is the centrality around
which all of Christianity turns.
—David Rhys Jones

To forgive is defined as (1) giving up resentment of or claim to requital, and (2) to cease to feel resentment against. These two aspects of the definition are actually two different issues of forgiveness. You can give up resentment of or claim to requital and yet still feel resentment against another. The issue of requital (compensation or retaliation), making another "pay" for their wrong, can be given up, while feelings of resentment against an offender can continue. Conversely, you may cease to feel resentment toward an offender and still seek requital as a form of "justice."

In the *Journal of Psychology and Theology*, Jared Pingleton describes the theological function of forgiveness: "Forgiveness is necessitated whenever one sustains a violation of their sense of justice or fairness. Simply defined, forgiveness can be conceptualized as 'giving up one's right to hurt back.' This operational definition recognizes, anticipates and attempts to mitigate against the *lex talionis*, or 'law of the talon'—the human organism's universal, almost reflexive propensity for retaliation and retribution in the face of hurt and pain at the hand of another."[22]

Jesus stood in opposition to the *lex talionis* when He said that His followers should forgive unconditionally. When Peter asked Jesus how many times he needed to forgive his brother or sister who sinned against him, he suggested what he probably thought a generous number—seven. Jesus said, "I do not say to you, up to seven times, but up to seventy times seven" (Matthew 18:22). Four hundred and ninety times? Jesus was probably not telling Peter to keep track of how many times he forgave, or that he could stop forgiving the four hundred ninety-first time. Jesus was teaching the principle that His followers are to be forgivers who desire to live in unity with others.

Jesus was concerned enough about the fellowship of believers that He taught that if we don't forgive each other then God won't forgive us (Matthew 6:14–15). Jesus knew the human tendency is toward revenge, not forgiveness; therefore, He emphatically taught the importance of forgiveness.

There is a process to forgiveness. It is a complex phenomenon in response to the offensive event. An offended person moves through hurt, anger, and information-seeking stages before reaching the forgiveness stage—which consists of reframing, releasing the desire to retaliate, and wishing the offender well.[23]

Since forgiveness is a complex phenomenon encompassing

many dimensions of human experience, and since every human experience is different, it follows that every human's process of forgiveness will be different.

Forgiving and forgetting are separate processes, so the requirement to forget an offense should not be included in the forgiveness process. Scripture does not demand forgetting; it does demand forgiving. In *The Road Home*, Darrell Puls writes, "The challenge then is not to forgive and forget, but to remember and change. We don't want to remember because we fear the resurrection of buried pain, but the pain is the portal through which we must pass in order to forgive."[24] The process of forgiveness will be painful. However, it must be walked through in order to move beyond the pain to experience the ultimate freedom of forgiveness.

Forgiveness is the releasing of a debt; it is the relinquishment of the right to seek revenge. The offended can forgive their offender without the offender expressing remorse. The offended need not wait upon the offender to become remorseful before forgiveness is granted. The offender may never express remorse or seek forgiveness from the offended.

But you and I must forgive as is commanded in Scripture, regardless of the condition of the offender's heart. This unconditional forgiveness frees the offended from the pain of hurt, resentment, anger, and bitterness that would otherwise imprison them. Lewis Smedes wrote, "When we are the ones who have been hurt, we simply cannot afford to wait for the other person to come to his senses before we begin healing ourselves."[25] The first time I read this quote, the proverbial light bulb went off above my head. We must take responsibility for our own forgiveness and healing processes. We cannot give our offender the power to continue to hurt us by withholding our forgiveness. We must make the determination to forgive, and then we must follow Jesus' principles to do so. It will take a combination of willpower, spiritual fortitude, and prayer to forgive an unrepentant offender, but it is possible.

Reverend R.T. Kendall, minister of Westminster Chapel from 1977–2002, wrote, "Chances are high that those who hurt us don't even think they have done anything wrong. Nine of ten people I have to forgive don't think they have done anything wrong to me (that suggests that I, too, have probably hurt people without knowing)."

He went on to say, "I never went to them and told them I forgave them (this would have insulted them). It happened in my heart. Once you forgive in your heart, it ceases to be an issue whether they repent or not."[26]

Forgiving a penitent offender would appear to be easier than forgiving the unrepentant. "Forgiving the hardheaded, dry-eyed unrepentant is hard in deed," wrote Smedes. "And yet, when we realize that forgiving is the only remedy for the pain the offender left us with, the only way to heal the hurt he caused, we have an incentive to forgive no matter if his heart is hard as flint."[27]

Smedes gives six good reasons for forgiving people who wounded us even though they do not care or never say they are sorry. They are:

1. Forgiving is something good we do for ourselves; we should not have to wait for permission from the person who did something bad to us.

2. When we forgive someone who does not say he's sorry, we are not issuing him a welcome back to the relationship we had before; if he wants to come back, he must come in sorrow.

3. To give forgiveness requires nothing but a desire to be free of our resentment. To receive forgiveness requires sorrow for what we did to give someone reason to be resentful.

4. We cannot expect to be forgiven without sorrow for the wrong we did. We should not demand sorrow for the wrong someone did to us.

5. Repentance does not earn the right to forgiveness; it only prepares us to receive the gift.

6. A wounded person should not put her future happiness in the hands of the person who made her miserable.[28]

Determining to forgive the unrepentant offender facilitates the entire process of forgiveness. It allows the offended to obey the commands of God, become free from the detrimental emotional, spiritual, and physical effects of unforgiveness, move beyond the pain that the offense caused, and begin the process of being restored to wholeness.

It is important to separate the issues of forgiveness and reconciliation when considering the unremorseful offender. One can always choose to forgive. It takes two people in agreement to reconcile. Pope John Paul II knew the difference.

On May 31, 1981, while in St. Peter's Square, the pope was shot in the abdomen and hand and was seriously injured by Mehmet Ali Agca. The would-be assassin was sentenced to twenty-five years in prison. On December 27, 1983, Pope John Paul II visited Ali Agca in prison and forgave him for attempting to kill him. This story fascinated the world. The cover of the January 9, 1984, issue of *Time* magazine read, "Why Forgive?" showing an image of the pope shaking Ali Agca's hand. The cover story was subtitled, "A pardon from the Pontiff, a lesson in forgiveness for a troubled world."[29]

It would seem that the world should *expect* the pope to forgive his offender. Pope John Paul II did forgive him, yet two and a half years passed before they met. Did the process of forgiveness for the pope's forgiving an unrepentant offender take two and a half years? If so, the pope's example should present hope to those of us who struggle to forgive our offenders and feel that we are not capable of forgiveness or are not able to forgive quickly enough.

When I was writing this chapter, I remembered to read a book that I had been meaning to read. It is titled *I Was Wrong* by Jim Bakker. Anyone over the age of forty knows the story of Jim Bakker and PTL and the affair and the downfall. I think I assumed the book would tell Jim's side of the story, and it would justify his actions, and then he would say that he had been wrong about a few things, and that would be it. I was wrong!

At one time, this man was one of the most powerful, high-profile Christian leaders in the world. He fell hard, was sentenced to forty-five years in prison, had the sentence reduced to eighteen years, and served four and a half years. He admits his faults, asks for forgiveness, and grants forgiveness to some people whom I would have a very hard time saying a cordial word to . . . let alone forgiving.

The whole time Jim was in prison, he had an interesting question: "What did I do wrong?" Jim honestly believed that he did not commit the crimes for which he was in prison. Not that it mattered. He was in prison, and he determined to learn everything God wanted to teach him.

People came to visit and encourage him. Eventually, some of the people who helped put him in prison came to visit, and Jim asked them for their forgiveness. The entire time I was reading the book I kept asking, *How do you do that? How do you sit in prison, determine to study hard and learn what God allowed you to be put there to learn, admit your imperfections, and then forgive people who hurt you while you are still there?*

A partial answer to my questions was found when Jim quoted R.T. Kendall's book, *God Meant It for Good.* "If you are a Christian, there will come a day—it may be soon—when the unexpected, the unthinkable happens to you. Your immediate question will be 'God, why did you let this happen?' The temptation will be to let yourself be filled with bitterness, hatred, and desire for revenge . . . Sometimes, however, we are called upon to forgive people who refuse to acknowledge that they have even done anything wrong. And there are those who don't think they have done anything wrong. But you have to forgive them, too—they are the hardest people to forgive . . . It is one thing to say, 'I have forgiven him for what he did'—and we can say it and think we mean it—but it is another thing to truly and totally forgive."[30]

Jim Bakker was released from prison on July 1, 1994. There is an epilogue at the end of his book that says, "On July 22, 1996, shortly after Jim Bakker had completed the writing of this book, a federal jury ruled that PTL was not selling securities by offering Lifetime Partnerships at Heritage USA. The jury's ruling thus affirms what Jim Bakker had contended from the first day he was indicted and throughout this volume."[31]

In other words, Jim was innocent of the legal charges brought against him. Thus he was wrongly sent to prison. He freely admits that he did many things wrong, but he went to prison for crimes that the federal jury later ruled did not occur.

Gary and I met Jim when he was beginning to write the book. He was so completely broken that it was disturbing to see. He was uncomfortable around people, and he could not look anyone in the eye. Even today, he is often unsure of how people, especially Christian people, will react to him. Sadly, he has good reason to be skeptical.

Dr. Luke Holter was a guest on *The Jim Bakker Show*. He got on an airplane to fly home, and he was seated next to another passenger who started making small talk. The man asked Luke what he had been in town to do. Luke told him that he had been on Jim Bakker's TV show. The man's immediate reaction was, "Now there's a guy who has a lot to answer for." I love Luke's response. He said, "Yeah, well, so do you!"

Luke (who has a sharp mind *and* a PhD) went on to ask,

"What should we do? He went to prison. He has been broken. He asked for forgiveness. Should we kill him? Would that be enough?" Needless, to say, the man was quiet the rest of the flight.

Luke's question is poignant. What should we do? What should we do to our offenders? Should we make them suffer? Should we hurt them as badly as they hurt us? Should we kill them? Would that make us feel better? No, the best and only solution for the offended is to forgive.

Jesus would not have commanded us to forgive if we were not capable of forgiving. Forgiveness can take time, and restoration may never happen, but we must remember that God is working all things together for good to them who love Him and are called according to His purpose (Romans 8:28).

In the past, forgiveness was seen as a subject for the theologian and philosopher. However, in the last twenty years, it has become the subject of empirical research by psychologists. Recent psychological studies have shown a correlation between the ability to forgive and mental and physical well-being.[32]

> Make me understand the depth of Your forgiveness toward me so that I won't hold back forgiveness from others. I realize that my forgiving someone doesn't make them right; it makes me free.
>
> —STORMIE OMARTIAN[33]

That is an intellectual, textbook way of saying that psychologists have done case studies with real people, and they have found that people who forgive their offenders heal faster than those who don't forgive.

Refuse to give your offender the power over you that unforgiveness grants. The rise in blood pressure, tightness in the chest, and general feeling of anger that arises in me doesn't hurt my offender. It only hurts me. Forgiveness is a process, and it takes time. And when it comes to attempting to obey God's command to forgive, I will give Him all the time necessary. I hope that you will too.

Prayer

Forgive me, Father, for I have sinned. Knowing that You have forgiven me makes it mandatory for me to forgive others. I have sinned against You, God of the universe, and yet You choose to forgive me. Others have sinned against me, so help me to forgive them as completely as You forgive me.

The Promises of God

For if you forgive men their trespasses, your heavenly Father will also forgive you.

Matthew 6:14

Judge not, and you shall not be judged. Condemn not, and you shall not be condemned. Forgive, and you will be forgiven.

Luke 6:37

Smart people know how to hold their tongue; their grandeur is to forgive and forget.

Proverbs 19:11 MSG

The LORD says, "Forget what happened before, and do not think about the past. Look at the new thing I am going to do . . . I will make a road in the desert and rivers in the dry land."

Isaiah 43:18–19 NCV

Therefore if you bring your gift to the altar, and there remember that your brother has something against you, leave your gift there before the altar, and go your way. First be reconciled to your brother, and then come and offer your gift.

Matthew 5:23–24

Chapter 6

Love Your Neighbor

And the second [commandment], like it, is this:
"You shall love your neighbor as yourself."
—Mark 12:31

In the early 1990s, I had the privilege of touring with author and speaker Tony Campolo. Tony tells the story of a man who had a great impact on his life as a boy. When the man was older and had suffered a stroke, Tony went to visit him in the hospital. Tony told him about his many travels, where he had been speaking recently, and how busy his schedule kept him. The man spoke a few words that Tony said changed his life. He said, "You go all over the world speaking to people who, ten years from now, won't remember your name, and you haven't any time left for the people who really care about you."[34]

Who really cares about you? If you cannot answer that question because you feel as if no one cares for you or loves you, then you have missed a very important point in this book. God loves you! He loves you much so that He gave His only Son as the payment for your sins. That is the greatest love that has ever been known and shown in the course of human history. And it is directed at you! So I hope that even if you cannot come up with one name of a person who loves and cares about you, you will know that God loves you.

Most of us can think of at least one person who loves us. You may think of the name of a spouse, child, parent, relative, or friend. Most people will think of the names of many people who love them. The question raised by Jesus' command to love your neighbor as yourself is: "Do you love the people who love you as much as you love yourself?" And to take the term *neighbor* further, "Do you love the people who *do not* love you as you love yourself?"

When Gary started singing in the show, there were two coworkers in particular with whom he felt like he would become friends. Denny had been a young pastor when his wife had an affair and left him. This experience, along with the ups and downs of life, had left him bitter and estranged from God. Paul had lived a rough life, but he knew about God. He didn't have a relationship with Him, but like a lot of good ol' boys, he thought things were fine between him and " the Good Lord." Yet his life was going downhill fast.

Gary didn't preach to the guys backstage. He didn't raise his eyebrows when they were involved in questionable situations. He simply lived his life. He came to work with a great attitude, did his job, laughed and joked, and was one of the guys. Within a few weeks, Gary noticed that Denny's dusty old Bible was being pulled out and read. There also didn't seem to be quite as many vices backstage as there had once been.

Three years later, Paul left the show. Gary felt as though he had let God down because Paul's life did not seem to be any different than it had been. It was a couple of years later that Gary was driving home after the evening show around Christmastime. It was late, and I had asked him to stop by the grocery store to pick up a few things on his way home. The parking lot at the store was almost empty when Gary pulled in. Across the lot, he noticed a familiar pickup truck with an arm waving out the window for Gary to come over to him. It was Paul.

Gary drove over and got into Paul's truck. They started talking, and Paul said, "I want you to know that I've rededicated my life to the Lord, and you have a lot to do with that. The whole time we worked together you knew what I was doing, and how I was living, but you never looked down on me. You just loved me, and I thank you for that." Gary came home and told me the story, and he finished it with, "That's the greatest Christmas present that I could have gotten."

Denny left the show a couple of years later. Gary got to see the changes God made in Denny's life while they worked together. After years of heartache and bitterness, Denny allowed God to soften his heart, and the difference in his life, attitude, and countenance is obvious. He is married to a wonderful lady, lives near and sings with his children and grandchildren, leads worship at his church, and has a new outlook on life. Gary was used by our loving Savior to love someone who needed to be loved. His willingness to be used may have opened the door to a heart that had been locked for many years. Denny later told us, "God brought you to Branson, and I was one of the reasons why."

Loving others as you love yourself allows you to be selfless, rather than selfish. Some of the most miserable people you will ever meet are the most selfish. If you live for yourself, you will be discontented, self-absorbed, restless, and insecure. It doesn't matter how successful you think you are or how much money you have or how self-satisfied you pretend to be. If getting what you want is more important than giving others what they need, you will always be dissatisfied. Jesus said, "For whoever desires to save his life will lose it, but whoever loses his life for My sake will find it" (Matthew 16:25). If we follow Jesus Christ, we give up our lives (our ambitions, desires, and plans) for the sake of Christ, and then we find life. Conversely, if you decide to pursue your own selfish ambitions, desires, and plans at the expense of following Jesus and doing the things that He says are important—things like loving your neighbor as you much as you love yourself—you will lose your life. Concerning losing and finding life, Jesus is not speaking literally. He is speaking figuratively, meaning that you will lose the best, most fulfilling, most satisfying aspects of life because you attempted to live it your way rather than His way.

Jesus then said that the second greatest commandment is to love your neighbor as yourself. How do you love your neighbor as yourself? The Golden Rule may be a good place to start: "Do to others as you would have them to do to you" (Luke 6:31 NIV). How many of life's problems would never exist if this rule for interpersonal relationships were followed? How many marriages would be saved if spouses lived by it? How many bitter vendettas would never have existed? How many wars would never have been waged?

There is an adage in counseling that says, "Feelings follow actions." This means that if you act as if you feel a certain way, there is an excellent chance that, in the future, you actually *will* feel that way. If you act as though you care about someone, rather than acting as though you don't, you will begin to genuinely care. This is usually the result of your heart experiencing a change because you get to know someone well enough to begin seeing life from their perspective.

My mother-in-law, Sandy, has a gift for caring about people. Everywhere she goes her warm, Italian personality draws people to her. Within minutes of meeting someone, she is talking with them, and usually crying with them, about a difficult situation that the former stranger is experiencing. It's amazing to watch! We walk into the lobby at our church and women she has not seen in months (and probably only met once on a visit) come running over to give her an update on their situation. When Sandy says she is stopping by the ladies' room, everyone in the family knows to have a seat because she will always end up talking to another lady there who is going through a problem, and it may take awhile.

Sandy genuinely cares about people. It's sad to think that the reason she has such an impact on people could be that there are so few people who *do* care about others. And maybe when you meet someone who really does care, like Sandy, it is so refreshing that you spill your guts to a stranger.

One of the reasons that loving and giving to others during a time of hurt is so important is because self-pity and selfishness will destroy an emotionally distraught person with quick precision. Wallowing in self-pity or being self-absorbed can result in becoming withdrawn and overly introspective. There is a time for stepping back and taking a good, long look at life, but if you begin to feel depression, extreme anxiety, or panic, you should seek help.

During a time of sadness, hurt, tragedy, and any other circumstance that causes pain, it is very important to attempt to stay involved in your day-to-day activities. You can allow yourself some time to cry, but don't keep crying. Don't sink into a pit of despair or superficially pretend that nothing is wrong. Both extremes are to be avoided. Feel the pain, and pray for comfort. Get up and do what you ought to do, and pray for God to teach you what you need to learn through the pain.

One of my favorite illustrations of the forgiveness process that leads to loving one's neighbor/offender is in the Victor Hugo classic *Les Misérables*. The bishop, Monseigneur Bienvenu, welcomes a just-released prison inmate, Jean Valjean, into his home. The bishop gives Jean Valjean a meal and a bed to sleep in. During the night, Jean Valjean robs the priest of some valuable silver objects, dropping a basket that holds the items as he flees over the garden wall. In the morning while working in his garden, the bishop finds the basket and knows that Jean Valjean has robbed him.

The bishop's actions that follow are astonishing. After discovering that his kindness has resulted in his being robbed, he keeps working in his garden and has his breakfast. And he also apparently decides to forgive Jean Valjean.

As he finishes breakfast, the gendarmes (police) bang on the bishop's door with a red-handed Jean Valjean in custody. When confronted with his offender, the bishop says, "Ah, there you are! I am glad to see you. But! I gave you the candlesticks also, which are silver like the rest. Why did you not take them along with your plates?"

Stunned, Jean Valjean is released by the gendarmes when the bishop explains that he had not stolen the silver. Then the bishop goes to the mantel, takes down the silver candlesticks, and gives them to his offender. And then in one of the most beautiful statements of forgiveness ever written, the bishop says, "Jean Valjean, my brother: you no longer belong to evil, but to good. It is your soul that I am buying for you. I withdraw it from dark thoughts and from the spirit of perdition and I give it to God!"

The bishop knew one of the principles of forgiveness—empathy toward the offender. Yes, you read that correctly . . . the offender. There are times when a crime or wrong is so horrendous that empathy with the offender is not required or possible. In lesser cases of offense, however, it is helpful in the forgiveness process for the offended person to attempt to empathize with the offender, in order to try to understand how the wrong occurred. It may be useful to ask questions such as: What happened to my offender that would cause him to hurt me in such a way? What made him or her think that doing what

> Lord, it's very difficult for me to love this person, but I'm going to trust You to love him (or her) through me, because in my own natural abilities and capacities, I'm unable to do it.
>
> —CHARLES STANLEY[35]

they did to me was okay? What caused my offender to become so self-serving and self-absorbed that they would not consider the action done to me as sinful or hurtful or wrong? It is often helpful to "walk a mile someone else's shoes" when walking through the forgiveness process.

How different would our world be if we forgave as quickly and loved our neighbor as thoroughly as the bishop? How much less stress, strain, and bitterness would we encounter if we acknowledged our being wronged, forgave our offender, and never gave it another thought? Jesus said that we are to love our neighbor as much as we love ourselves (Matthew 22:39). It is humanly very difficult, but "I can do all things through Christ who strengthens me" (Philippians 4:13).

Prayer

God, today is the day that I am releasing bitterness, anger, and resentment over a hurtful situation. Soften my heart, and let Your peace that passes understanding comfort me any time I feel those familiar resentful feelings. I acknowledge that I have been wronged, but I do not want to live in bondage to my offender through unforgiveness. Help me to love my neighbor, and even my enemy. This will take a supernatural work in me through the power of Your Holy Spirit, but I'm willing to let You do the work. In Jesus' name I pray.

The Promises of God

Love your enemies, bless those who curse you, do good to those who hate you, and pray for those who spitefully use you and persecute you, that you may be sons of your Father in heaven.

Matthew 5:44–45

So be careful! If another follower sins, warn him, and if he is sorry and stops sinning, forgive him. If he sins against you seven times in one day and says that he is sorry each time, forgive him.

Luke 17:3–4 NCV

Don't get angry. Don't be upset; it only leads to trouble.

Psalm 37:8 NCV

Chapter 7

Move On

*Embracing what God does for you is the best thing you can do
for him. Don't become so well-adjusted to your culture that
you fit into it without even thinking. Instead, fix your attention
on God. You'll be changed from the inside out.*

—Romans 12:2 MSG

You cannot move on until you have let go of the past. It isn't
enough to love your neighbor. Christians are also commanded to love our enemies. Jesus said, "But I say to you, love
your enemies, bless those who curse you, do good to those who
hate you, and pray for those who spitefully use you and persecute you" (Matthew 5:44). I have this summary of the verse
scribbled in my journal, but I don't know where I found it, so
my apologies to its author. My journal note summarizes it this
way: (1) Love your enemies, (2) Bless those who curse you,
(3) Do good to haters, and (4) Pray for users and persecutors.

This note is a perfect example of how countercultural it is to
be a Christian. Our leader is telling us to do exactly the opposite

of what the secular theories of human interaction teach. There is no "Look out for Number One," "Stick it to the man," or "Claw your way to the top" philosophy with Jesus. He tells us to treat the people who mistreat us with love. How the heck are we supposed to do that?

For me personally, it means doing several specific things. First, I try not to talk about my offender. (This is ironic because writing this book in the hopes of helping others has forced me to talk about the situation.) Proverbs 13:3 says, "He who guards his mouth preserves his life, but he who opens wide his lips shall have destruction." This can be hard to do. We live in a very small town, and everyone knows everyone else's business, including the fact that we were fired. So I have to be prepared to run into people everywhere I go, and they often (innocently and lovingly) want to know what happened. And then there are also the people who want to share with us their opinion of what happened and why.

> Beneath all the layers of sin and hurtful actions is a person made in the image of God—a person in need of the same redemption graciously bestowed upon you and me. The challenge is to keep that perspective at all times, remembering with humility that we, too, are in need of a Savior.
>
> —CHARLES STANLEY[37]

I find that these conversations set me back in my forgiveness process, so I try to avoid them. I change the subject and talk about what's happening now, not what happened in the past. Most people understand and the subject is changed or dropped. Standing in the grocery store and talking trash is not going to do me any good.

Second, I have tried to empathize with my offender (as recommended in the previous chapter). The greatest help to me in empathizing with my offender has been the realization that God used him to accomplish His will in our lives. If God can harden Pharaoh's heart in order to free His people from slavery, and if God can send an evil spirit to torment King Saul because the kingdom of Israel had been taken from him because of disobedience, He can surely do whatever He deems necessary to accomplish His will. It has been confirmed to us repeatedly that God's will was accomplished for us. It wasn't what we expected, and it wasn't done the way we would have wanted, but we now believe and know that God had a different plan for us, and we needed to be moved into it. Look and listen for confirmation that God has allowed a situation because He has a bigger, better plan for your life.

Third, Gary and I felt that we could not seek retribution for wrongs committed against us. We did not come to this conclusion immediately, but after making it a matter of prayer, we felt that we were directed to place justice for our situation completely in God's hands. To make a long story short, we sought legal counsel and were advised to file two lawsuits to remedy the situation. Gary and I discussed our options and decided that we didn't have peace in our spirits about the possible lawsuits.

We knew that 1 Corinthians 6 says that a Christian brother should not sue another brother, and Christians are supposed to work out their disagreements within the church (Matthew 18:15–17). We requested several meetings, one of which was to be an arbitration meeting with both parties and our pastors. These requests were denied. So now we had a major decision to make: *Do we pursue legal action or not?*

In what I believe to be a directive from the Lord, I was reading Ron Steele's book about Reinhard Bonnke, *Plundering Hell to Populate Heaven*. In it Steele tells the story of a time in Bonnke's ministry when he needed a lawyer. It read, "He wondered what lawyer he could get. Then, slowly, he bowed his head and prayed, 'Lord Jesus, You are my lawyer. I put this case in Your hands.'"[36] These words jumped off the page at me! Our lawyers were supposed to be good, but they weren't as good as Jesus, so we chose to retain the legal firm of Father, Son, and Holy Spirit, Esquire!

Obeying God means leaving vengeance in His hands. Isaiah 1 gives a list of things to do to live an obedient life. Two of the items are to seek justice and punish those who do wrong to others. Proverbs 31:8 says to speak up for those who cannot speak for themselves. We are to defend the defenseless, but we are *not* to defend *ourselves*.

This is a tough one for me! The fact is that Scripture does *not* say to punish those who do wrong to you. It says exactly the opposite:

> *"If someone does wrong to you, do not pay him back by doing wrong to him. Try to do what everyone thinks is right. Do your best to live in peace with everyone. My friends, do not try to punish others when*

they wrong you, but wait for God to punish them with his anger. It is written, 'I will punish those who do wrong; I will repay them,' says the Lord" (Romans 12:17–19 NCV).

Take the high road. Be the bigger person. "Do to others what you would want them to do to you" (Luke 6:31 NCV). Don't do to others what they *have* done to you. There is not a better example of someone deserving to take revenge than that of David and Saul. David had been a loyal servant and soldier for Saul, and because of jealousy, Saul turned against David and chased him for years with the intent of killing him.

In spite of all of this, David said to Saul, "May the LORD judge between us, and may he punish you for the wrong you have done to me! But I am not against you. There is an old saying: 'Evil things come from evil people.' But I am not against you . . . May the LORD be our judge and decide between you and me. May he support me and show that I am right. May he save me from you" (1 Samuel 24:12–15 NCV).

Let no mean or low thought have a moment's place in my mind . . . Let me face adversity with courage . . . Give me grace this day for faith to put my own trust in love, rather than in force, when other men harden their hearts against me. Rid my heart of all vain anxieties and paralyzing fears. Give me a cheerful and buoyant spirit, and peace in doing Your will, for Christ's sake.

—JOHN BAILLIE[40]

We must be willing to do the same. We have to believe God will take care of us. One of the attributes of God is justice. God is just, so at some point, He will right all wrongs. He will repay.

I can tell you with certainty that we know God has blessed us as a result of our decision to obey His command. I will not say that we have not struggled, but we are blessed beyond measure in our family, church, home, and ministry.

Fourth (and hardest, I must admit), I have had to pray for my offender. This is hard for anyone, especially if you feel that your offender is not experiencing the justice that he should be. Attempting to reconcile justice and the offense can be a downward spiral of confusion and anger, and it can certainly impede, if not stop, your healing.

> Everything that was done to me or that I have done which causes me pain, I surrender to You. May it no longer torment me or affect what I do today.
>
> —STORMIE OMARTIAN[41]

In spite of what has occurred, pray that the offender comes into a relationship with God, and then let God deal with the discipline that may need to occur. Hebrews 12:6 states that God disciplines His own child. Matthew Henry's commentary on this passage says that God may let others alone in their sins, but He will correct sin in His own children.

We must move on. We must get past our hurt and move toward hope. We cannot allow bitterness and resentment to rob us of our joy and happiness. I read a sobering quote that said, "Resentment is like taking poison and waiting for the other person to die."[38] We must not allow resentment to poison us. We are hurting no one but ourselves because, sadly, most of our offenders haven't given us a second thought. We would like to think they are remorseful and can't get over the loss that they have caused. We may fantasize about saying to them what Drew Barrymore's Cinderella character in the movie *Ever After* says to her wicked stepmother: "I want you to know that I will forget you after this moment, and never think of you again. But you, I am quite certain, will think about me every single day for the rest of your life."[39] But chances are, they won't. So the only advice I can give is what I've had to do myself: don't talk about it (and continue to live in the past hurt), try to empathize with your offender, don't seek retribution, and pray.

It is hard for me to relive this situation, even to write about it. I'm writing my thoughts and feelings in order to possibly help someone else who has been hurt, but God is still healing my heart. Gary has been much more rational and quicker to forgive than I have been. My forgiveness process is ongoing, but I've come a long way. I can now honestly pray this prayer: "God, I believe that our unexpected course change has put us on the path that You want us to walk. We have all of the blessings that we could ever hope for and dream of. Thank You for moving us where you want us to be. I trust You."

Recently a speaker used an illustration that I've thought of many times while going through the forgiveness process. He said that he could see people coming to the altar, and they were spiritually burdened with a heavy load of cinder blocks and chains. These blocks and chains represented problems, addictions, heartache, sin, and disappointment. They came to the altar, prayed for God's deliverance, and as they were set free, the blocks and chains fell off. After they had finished praying and rejoicing over their freedom, sadly and robotically, they bent down and picked up the blocks and chains and carried them out. God forbid that we continue to carry a load of bitterness and resentment when He can lead us to forgiveness, freedom, and a release of our burdens, if we will allow Him to work in our lives. It's time to move on . . .

Prayer

God, I pray that *You* will stop *me* from dwelling on the wrong that was done to me. I do not want to think about how wrong my offender is and what I think should be done for justice to be accomplished. Please make the words of my mouth and the thoughts of my heart acceptable to You (Psalm 19:14). I want my actions to be pleasing to You, so help me to obey the voice of Your Holy Spirit when He says, "This is the way, walk in it" (Isaiah 30:21).

The Promises of God

He says, "Don't be afraid, because I have saved you. I have called you by name, and you are mine. When you pass through the waters, I will be with you. When you cross rivers, you will not drown. When you walk through fire, you will not be burned, nor will the flames hurt you."

Isaiah 43:1–2 NCV

Don't be happy when your enemy is defeated.

Proverbs 24:17 NCV

Don't say, "I will get even for this wrong." Wait for the LORD to handle the matter.

Proverbs 20:22 NLT

I give new life to those who are humble and to those whose hearts are broken.

Isaiah 57:15 NCV

Summing up: Be agreeable, be sympathetic, be loving, be compassionate, be humble. That goes for all of you, no exceptions. No retaliation. No sharp-tongued sarcasm. Instead, bless—that's your job, to bless. You'll be a blessing and also get a blessing.

1 Peter 3:8–9 MSG

I, the LORD, love justice. I hate stealing and everything that is wrong. I will be fair and give my people what they should have, and I will make an agreement with them that will continue forever.

Isaiah 61:8 NCV

The LORD does what is right and fair for all who are wronged by others.

Psalm 103:6 NCV

Part Three

FEAR NOT,
ONLY BELIEVE

*I don't know what we're going to do, but I do know
what we're not going to do. We're not going to be afraid.
We're going to stand still. And we're going to see the
deliverance of the Lord . . . And God delivered.*

—Mark Batterson[42]

Recently an opportunity for Gary came up that appeared to be the *perfect* situation for him. It seemed like God may have been answering a huge prayer. Gary went out for a few hours to run errands, and I was cheerfully cleaning the house and telling God all of the reasons that a "yes" answer to this prayer was the right answer.

When Gary called to tell me that the answer was "No," I calmly tried to say all of the encouraging things a wife is supposed to say when her husband experiences disappointment.

But when I hung up the phone, I physically fell over the top of the island in the kitchen and started sobbing uncontrollably. It was as if a rushing river of sadness was released through a hole in the dam of bravery that I had tried to keep plugged up.

And then I heard the voice of the Lord. It was not His audible voice, but it was a complete sentence that I "heard" so loudly that I immediately stopped sobbing and stood up. He asked, "Do you trust Me?" I stood there stunned for a moment, trying to decide if I had heard Him with my ears. I think it was only in my heart, but I answered audibly, "Yes."

> Don't be afraid. Just stand still and watch the Lord rescue you today. The Egyptians [enemies, problems, circumstances] you see today will never be seen again. The Lord himself will fight for you. Just stay calm.
> —EXODUS 14:13–14 NLT

That was it. That's all that happened, but my attitude, day, and life were changed forever. I had told the Lord that I trusted Him, and I was certainly going to do it. Or at least attempt to do it. Trusting Him, believing Him, and not fearing circumstances are daily decisions to make, but I told Him I would trust Him, so I keep trying.

I cannot count the many times since that day that I have experienced another disappointment, but my mind goes back to the day when I said, "Yes," and then I can believe that each new disappointment was not God's best for my life. In my human wisdom, I have thought that several of them would have been fabulous, but apparently God didn't. So now I can't wait to see what He does!

Chapter 8

Have Faith

I recorded the song "Faith" in 1989, and the song's message is still imprinted in my heart and mind today.

When the future starts to look a little grim
And you're weary 'cause your faith is wearing thin
And that ray of hope somehow just won't shine through
Never giving up is all we have to do

'Cause faith can move the highest mountain
Turn deserts into fountains
Part the mighty waters of the deepest sea
Faith can make a broken heart mend
Bring the rain from heaven
Faith can even change the course of history

Trouble comes and you can't help but be afraid
Fear can only be the lack of having faith
Keep believing it won't get the best of you
Disappointment will soon disappear from view

And when it seems your dreams are falling down around you
Your faith can pick you and make them all come true[43]

These lyrics capture the hopelessness and desperation that can overcome us when we are going through times of discouragement, pain, and hurt. And then they give the answer to large problems with a small, five-letter word . . . *faith*.

The word *faith* is used frequently, and many times it has nothing to do with the biblical term. Organizations can be referred to as being "faith-based"; a person with any type of spirituality can be called "a person of faith"; or faith can be used to convey a sense of optimism, as in "she has faith in his ability to be a good father." While those are fine descriptions, *faith* can mean much more. According to Hebrews 11:1, "faith is the substance of things hoped for, the evidence of things not seen." This note in *The Woman's Study Bible* on Hebrews 11:1 provides insight:

> [Faith] is defined by two words: "substance" [Gk. *hupostasis*, lit. "that which stands under"] and "evidence" [Gk. *elenchos*, lit. "proof"]. Faith then is the foundation for the Christian life and the means by which all unseen things are tested. "Faith" is the nominal form of the verb "to believe" [Gk. *pisteuein*]. Faith, therefore, means trust or confidence in what God has promised, resulting in a life of faithfulness and perseverance. Faith is the only essential response to the grace of God (Heb. 11:6). Justification is the result of that faith.[44]

Based on this information, faith is two things: substance and evidence. First, as substance, faith is the foundation for the Christian life. Faith in the sacrificial gift of the blood of Christ as the remission for sins is the requirement for becoming a Christian. We are forgiven and sanctified (set apart as holy, purified) by faith in Christ's redemptive work. Faith is foundational to the Christian life because the righteousness of God is revealed "from faith to faith" (Romans 1:17).

What an interesting phrase, "from faith to faith." The first act of faith we must accomplish is to believe that Jesus Christ died for our sins, confess them, accept His forgiveness, and begin walking the path of faith. It seems logical that the last act of faith in life would be confidence in Christ's being the hope of glory (Colossians 1:27)—that is, our eternal salvation. Between those two acts of faith, we live out the daily Christian walk from faith to faith.

> We need faith to follow—daily! What worked yesterday may not be for today.
> —F.B. MEYER[47]

Second, faith is the evidence of things not seen. Having faith in God (believing who He said He is, believing He will do what He said He will do) helps us be faithful. Faith in God helps us persevere. It makes us steadfast when we should fall. It makes us confident when we should be broken. Faith encourages us to do what God said to do and trust Him to bring about the correct result.

Hebrews 11 is sometimes called "The Faith Hall of Fame" because it lists the names of the giants of faith and what they did to be inducted into this chapter. Then Hebrews 12:1–2 gives the reason for remembering what these giants of faith did:

Therefore we also, since we are surrounded by so great a cloud of witnesses, let us lay aside every weight, and the sin which so easily ensnares us, and let us run with endurance the race that is set before us, looking unto Jesus, the author and finisher of our faith, who for the joy that was set before Him endured the cross, despising the shame, and has sat down at the right hand of the throne of God.

We are encouraged to remember what those great men and women of faith did, to be encouraged by their examples, and to run our races by looking to Jesus! That's how we can be faith-full.

In moving through a time of hurt, it can be difficult to be full of faith, but it is imperative that we try to be faithful in spite of our feelings. Here's why: "Steadfast loyalty and unwavering trust are considered essential virtues for personal and spiritual growth."[45] And personal and spiritual growth are necessary when you walk faith to faith through sadness, disappointment, heartache, anger, sickness, tragedy, or any other circumstance that is beyond your ability to handle.

> It is not that we cannot stagger, but that we must not stagger in staggering situations.
>
> —REINHARD BONNKE[48]

The alternative to walking faith to faith is living fear to fear. Fear and its accompanying emotions of worry and doubt are killers. Scripture is full of admonitions to *fear not* because God knows that humans are prone to fear. I'm certain that this is one of the reasons that *fear not* was one of my directives in moving out of my hurt. God knew I would be fearful, and that I would worry, but

He wanted me to *fear not* by placing my trust in His Word. It's impossible to worry and trust God at the same time, so a willful choice must be made to trust, rather than to fear.

Tim was a Vietnam veteran who lived in Branson. He had been injured in Vietnam and was wheelchair bound. His spirit, however, was joyful, and he loved wheeling around Branson, talking to people and seeing shows. Gary spent countless hours at the Golden Corral talking and laughing with Tim. Tim passed away a couple of years after we met him, and at his funeral I met his sister, Cindy.

Cindy is a beautiful lady who radiates love, and her personality is infectious. I was stunned to learn that one month before her brother's funeral, Cindy's husband and two sons (both in their early twenties) had been killed in an auto accident. Cindy's life as she had known it was over. The men in her life whom she loved more than anyone or anything else on earth were gone.

Cindy will never know *why* these handsome, godly men were killed. She does not live a single day without thinking of them and missing them. Yet Cindy has faith and a confidence in the providence of God that is beyond normal human capacity. She isn't angry or bitter. In fact, she has turned something that could have caused her to lose her faith into one of the greatest testimonies of God's restorative power that I have ever heard. Cindy is continuing a ministry to young people that her sons started in the barn behind their house. At any time, she may have five college students living in her home, working in the ministry, and traveling with her as she shares her testimony around the world.

Last year, we ran into Cindy. She told me that the Lord had been bringing my face before her in prayer recently, so it was not a coincidence that we had run into each other. At a time when I needed *something* to help me know that God still knew I existed, He sent Cindy to encourage me. She gave me a book that she said had helped her. It was the book on faith that I mentioned earlier titled *Plundering Hell to Populate Heaven*. She said I should learn everything that I could from the book because she believed God was preparing Gary and me for something great.

So I read the book, and it strengthened my faith. It encouraged me to step outside of the comfort zone I had been living in and be open to attempting something new and different. When I finished the book, I prayed a prayer that Bonnke had prayed: "Lord, I want to be a person of faith if You are prepared to trust me."[46] I challenge you to pray that prayer, to allow your faith to be strengthened and your life to be changed.

Being "faith-full" has helped me move from hurt to hope. One of the ways this has been accomplished is by learning, knowing, and believing the promises of God. The promises of God are His Word to us. We can trust them.

> Give me grace, I ask, to understand the meaning of affliction and disappointment as I'm called on to endure. Deliver me from all fretfulness. Let me be wise to draw from every dispensation of Your providence the lesson You are teaching me.
>
> —JOHN BAILLIE[49]

God keeps His promises. Every promise that God made to the Israelites came true (Joshua 21:45).

Each chapter in this book has contained promises that will help you walk from faith to faith. Speak the promises of God out loud. Pray them. Hearing them spoken helps us believe them: "So then faith comes by hearing, and hearing by the word of God" (Romans 10:17). We are saved through faith (Ephesians 2:8), and we live daily and eternally by faith (Hebrews 11) because God *is* faithful.

Prayer

God, I'm feeling the burden of _____ today, so give me a believing heart and the faith to cast all of my burdens on You. Bring me peace and comfort through Your Holy Spirit. Lord, I give myself completely to You. Please make me strong. May my Lord Jesus Christ Himself and God my Father encourage me and strengthen me in every good thing I do and say (2 Thessalonians 2:16–17). I will not fear, for You are with me; I won't be dismayed, for You are my God. You will strengthen me, yes, You will help me, for You will uphold me with Your righteous right hand (Isaiah 41:10). Thank you, Jesus. In Your name I pray, amen.

The Promises of God

So people receive God's promise by having faith.

Romans 4:16 NCV

For by grace you have been saved through faith, and that not of yourselves, it is the gift of God, not of works, lest anyone should boast.

Ephesians 2:8–9

But the Lord is faithful. He will establish you and guard you against the evil one.

2 Thessalonians 3:3 ESV

Surely your goodness and unfailing love will pursue me all the days of my life, and I will live in the house of the LORD forever.

Psalm 23:6 NLT

I bow before your holy Temple as I worship. I praise your name for your unfailing love and faithfulness; for your promises are backed by all the honor of your name.

Psalm 138:2 NLT

The LORD searches all the earth for people who have given themselves completely to him. He wants to make them strong.

2 Chronicles 16:9 NCV

As soon as I pray, you answer me; you encourage me by giving me strength.

Psalm 138:3 NLT

The LORD is my shepherd; I shall not want.

Psalm 23:1 KJV

The LORD will make you like the head and not like the tail; you will be on top and not on bottom. But you must obey the commands of the LORD your God that I am giving you today, being careful to keep them.

Deuteronomy 28:13 NCV

And my God will supply all your needs according to His riches in glory by Christ Jesus.

Philippians 4:19 NASB

Yet in all these things we are more than conquerors through Him who loved us.

Romans 8:37

When you go to war against your enemies and you see horses and chariots and an army that is bigger than yours, don't be afraid of them. The LORD your God, who brought you out of Egypt, will be with you.

Deuteronomy 20:1 NCV

Greater is he that is in you, than he that is in the world.

1 John 4:4 KJV

And God can give you more than blessings than you need. Then you will always have plenty of everything— enough to give to every good work.

2 Corinthians 9:8 NCV

If you ask me for anything in my name, I will do it.

John 14:14 NCV

"So no weapon that is used against you will defeat you. You will show that those who speak against you are wrong. These are the good things my servants receive. Their victory comes from me," says the LORD.

Isaiah 54:17 NCV

Heal me, LORD, and I will be healed; save me, and I will be saved, for you are the one I praise.

Jeremiah 17:14 NIV

Cast your cares on the LORD and he will sustain you; he will never let the righteous be shaken.

Psalm 55:22 NIV

Is anyone among you suffering? Let him pray. Is anyone cheerful? Let him sing psalms. Is anyone among you sick? Let him call for the elders of the church, and let them pray over him, anointing him with oil in the name of the Lord. And the prayer of faith will save the sick, and the Lord will raise him up. And if he has committed sins, he will be forgiven.

James 5:13–15

Chapter 9

Hope in God

*The consolations of God are strong enough to support his peo-
ple under their heaviest trials . . . The free grace of God, the
merits and mediation of Christ, and the powerful influences
of his Spirit, are the grounds of this [gospel] hope, and so it is
a steadfast hope. Christ is the object and ground of the believer's hope.*

—Matthew Henry's Concise Commentary on Hebrews 6:19 [50]

received this e-mail through my website:

> *I'm not really sure why I'm writing to you. I'm not an
> emotional person. I was cruising around YouTube
> and somehow clicked on one of your videos, "Not Too
> Far from Here." It felt like someone punched me in the
> stomach, and for a minute I actually forgot to breathe.*

> *I was never raised around the whole church or God-
> thing. Never really even gave it a second thought
> until recently. I've been handed a death sentence. No,*

I'm not in jail or anything. I've been diagnosed with glioblastoma, an inoperable brain tumor. They can treat it, but there is no cure. Going blind and deaf, and becoming incapable of remembering the simplest things, and eventually death is what I have to look forward to over the next 18 to 24 months.

So I have been questioning things I've never questioned. And then I came across that video, and on the first try, I find this page (for the website). I have been reading stuff online, but it is all so confusing and contradictory. I hate to bother you, but I don't really know anyone like this, and therefore can't really ask anyone. I guess my question is . . . Is God really real?

I broke down and sobbed. I had come into the office to start writing this chapter on hope. Hope in the darkest times. Hope when your world is falling apart. Hope when you received terrible news. Hope when you feel lost, rejected, and scorned. Hope when everything you thought your life would be is proven wrong.

I felt guilty. The trigger for writing this book was getting fired from a job—actually, getting fired from two jobs at the same time. It devastated us emotionally because it was so unexpected. It could ruin us financially. It has driven us to our knees. However, it didn't seem as devastating when compared to the diagnosis received by this girl named Danielle. Am I being immature? Selfish? Am I making too big a deal of my circumstance? While these are legitimate questions to ask, when you are hurting, you need hope. Hope to *get through* whatever has come into your life that you must now *walk through*.

In spite of what I was personally going through, I knew the answer to Danielle's question, so I answered her e-mail immediately:

> *Yes, God is real! He created everything, He made human beings to love Him, and then when we messed up, He sent His only Son to die for our sins, so that we could be forgiven. That's how much He loves you!!! That's why the end of the song you saw on YouTube says, "Jesus is waiting, not too far from here." If you ask Him to, God will make Himself real to you, and then you can be assured that He exists and He loves you. All of our physical bodies are dying, but our souls (that can communicate with God) live forever!*
>
> *Please continue to stay in contact with me. I hope that we can become friends. If you send me your address, I will send you a book that I wrote that will help you with your questions. The book is called,* There Is a God.
>
> *Kim*
>
> *P.S. Do you have a Bible? If not, I will send you one along with the book. Start reading it in the book of John. It will tell you the story of Jesus.*

Two weeks later, Gary and I were scheduled to sing at a church two hours from Danielle's home. I asked Danielle if she was able to come spend time with me while I was in the area. She said she would love to, so she drove two hours on that Sunday morning to meet me.

One thing you should know is that Danielle had never been

to church before. Imagine the bravery it took for her to make the trip to meet someone she had only spoken to by phone, and then to walk into a large church where she knew no one. That day, Danielle attended three services with us and went to lunch with my entire family, the pastor and his family, and church staff members. She came back to our hotel room and hung out with Gary and me. We talked at length about her cancer, her background, and the existence of God. I told her everything I could think of about salvation, Jesus Christ, and eternity. I was packing a whole bunch of information into one day because, quite honestly, I didn't know how much time she had left. It was staggering to me that a twenty-nine-year-old American woman could have grown up having no concept of the reality of God, having never been to church, or having never heard about Jesus and salvation.

When we said good-bye to Danielle late Sunday night, she hugged me and said, "This has been the best day of my life!" I was shocked. I had thought that perhaps I had come on too strong. Maybe I had given her too much information to process at once. But apparently, what we had given Danielle that day was love, acceptance, and hope.

Hope is absolutely essential on the journey from hurt to healing. Without hope, depression begins to take hold. Models for biblical counseling list sickness, death of a loved one, financial crisis, hormonal and/or chemical imbalance, bitterness, brooding, nursing a grudge, despair, worry, envy, disappointment, sorrow, guilt, and self-pity as beginning sources of depression. If you are severely depressed, please seek professional help. If, however, you are struggling with any of the above sources and need to know that there is hope, keep reading.

I have no platitudes to offer about hope. No "the grass is always greener on the other side." No "pull yourself up by your bootstraps." No "it's got to get better 'cause it can't get any worse" clichés. In fact, I have come to understand that "the 'dark night of the soul' . . . is one of the key means God uses to transform the human personality."[51] God allows us to be tested and tried in the fire, in order to be molded into His own image. We are supposed to count it all joy when we fall into various trials, knowing that the testing of our faith produces patience. "But let patience have its perfect work, that you may be perfect and complete, lacking nothing" (James 1:2–4).

Moving from hurt to healing will test our faith. We will be (or are being) tried by fire. We will have to endure with patience, but the promise is that if we allow patience to work in us, we will be made whole. We must not wallow in self-pity while we are being tried. There will be times that you just have to get up and do what you are supposed to do because that's all there is to do! There will be days when praying for strength is your lifeline. Sometimes we have to force ourselves to meditate on the Word of God because that's all we have to hold on to. In his classic book *Knowing God*, J.I. Packer writes that meditating on God's Word is "often a matter of arguing with oneself, reasoning oneself out of moods of doubt and unbelief into a clear apprehension of God's power and grace."[52] It is God's power and grace that will get us through to healing. We cannot do it in our own strength. If we could, we would have already done it.

I heard a wonderful speaker, Susan Allen, give a message titled, "A Certain Woman." Mark 5 tells the story of the woman who had been struggling with the issue of blood for twelve years. She heard that Jesus was coming to town, and she made it her priority to get to Him because she wanted to be healed. You know the story. She touches His clothing and is instantly healed! Jesus knew that healing virtue had gone out of Him, so He questioned who touched Him. She falls at his feet and tells Him she is the one who touched Him. He says, "Daughter, your faith has made you well. Go in peace, and be healed of your affliction" (v. 34).

Like I said, you know the story, but what Susan pointed out in her message is that this woman is described as a *certain* woman. I always assumed that this adjective described how she was a particular or specific woman. Susan asked us to think of what it would mean if the definition of *certain* in this case meant "not having any doubt about something: convinced or sure." What set her apart? What made her different? She was a *certain* woman: a purposeful, confident, sure, convinced, faith-filled woman who believed Jesus could do for her what she had heard He had done for others.

In her research, Susan found that over seventy times the Scripture pointed out a *certain* person: a certain scribe, a certain man, a certain centurion, a certain disciple, or a certain ruler. Certain meant purpose. So whether good or evil, the word certain was used to describe someone's identity.

Susan went on to describe herself as a *certain* woman. She has a purpose, and she spoke to a group of women about purpose.

One reason Susan's message hit me so strongly is because less than a year before she gave it, her twenty-four-year-old son had been killed on Easter Sunday in a freak accident. Susan said, "I am not *a* woman who lost her son. I am a *certain* woman who lost her son. I still wake up with a pain inside of me every day because I won't get to see my boy. But this Word that you put inside of you is for such a time as this."[53]

Susan was encouraging us to be *certain* women, and the message is for everyone. Men can be *certain* men. *Certain* parents raise *certain* children. *Certain* Christians know the purpose of life is to tell others what Jesus has done in our lives, and live life in such a way that they want the same kind of faith and hope that they see in *certain* men and *certain* women. We can only do this because we have hope.

Hope in a heavenly Father.

Hope in a Savior.

Hope in a Spirit of comfort and encouragement.

Hope is found in the Word of God and His promises and His faithfulness to fulfill them. My prayer is that you will be hopeful in knowing that God knows and cares about you and your circumstances. I pray you will be able to say what my friend, Cindy Cruse Ratcliff, said after five years of the heartache and disappointment of attempting unsuccessfully to have children. After she and her husband, Marcus, were blessed to adopt twins, she said, "You don't really know what's going on behind the scenes, but God has already gone before you and made a way for you. He worked everything out beautifully. He set us up to win."

With Jesus Christ, there is always hope!

Prayer

Lord, "Remember my suffering and my misery, my sorrow and trouble. Please remember me and think about me. But I have hope when I think of this: The LORD's love never ends; his mercies never stop. They are new every morning; LORD, your loyalty is great. I say to myself, 'The LORD is mine, so I hope in him.' The LORD is good to those who hope in him, to those who seek him. It is good to wait quietly for the LORD to save" (Lamentations 3:19–26 NCV).

"Hear my prayer, O LORD; listen to my plea! Answer me because you are faithful and righteous . . . I am losing all hope; I am paralyzed with fear. I remember the days of old. I ponder all your great works and think about what you have done. I lift my hands to you in prayer. I thirst for you as parched land thirsts for rain. Come quickly, LORD, and answer me, for my depression deepens. Don't turn away from me, or I will die. Let me hear of your unfailing love each morning, for I am trusting you. Show me where to walk, for I give myself to you. Rescue me from my enemies, LORD; I run to you to hide me. Teach me to do your will, for you are my God. May your gracious Spirit lead me forward on a firm footing" (Psalm 143:1, 4–10 NLT).

The Promises of God

Arise [from the depression and prostration in which circumstances have kept you—rise to a new life]! Shine [be radiant with the glory of the Lord], for your light has come, and the glory of the Lord has risen upon you!

Isaiah 60:1 AMP

So our hope is in the LORD. He is our help, our shield to protect us.

Psalm 33:20 NCV

Blessed are those who mourn, for they shall be comforted.

Matthew 5:4

Though I walk in the midst of trouble, You will revive me; You will stretch out Your hand against the wrath of my enemies, and Your right hand will save me.

Psalm 138:7

The hope of the righteous will be gladness, but the expectation of the wicked will perish.

Proverbs 10:28

Hope deferred makes the heart sick, but when the desire comes, it is a tree of life.

Proverbs 13:12

Let not your heart be troubled; you believe in God, believe also in Me.

John 14:1

Therefore humble yourselves under the mighty hand of God, that He may exalt you in due time, casting all your care upon Him, for He cares for you.

1 Peter 5:6–7

Be anxious for nothing, but in everything by prayer
and supplication, with thanksgiving, let your requests
be made known to God; and the peace of God, which
surpasses all understanding, will guard your hearts and
minds through Christ Jesus.

Philippians 4:6–7

Don't fret or worry. Instead of worrying, pray. Let peti-
tions and praises shape your worries into prayers, letting
God know your concerns. Before you know it, a sense of
God's wholeness, everything coming together for good,
will come and settle you down. It's wonderful what happens when Christ displaces worry at the center of your life.

Philippians 4:6–7 MSG

And my God shall supply all your need according to His
riches in glory by Christ Jesus.

Philippians 4:19

And the Lord will deliver me from every evil work and
preserve me for His heavenly kingdom. To Him be glory
forever and ever. Amen!

2 Timothy 4:18

He heals the brokenhearted and bandages their wounds.

Psalm 147:3 NLT

I find rest in God; only he gives me hope.

Psalm 62:5 NCV

Chapter 10

Seek God's Will

Not everyone who says to Me,
"Lord, Lord," shall enter the kingdom of heaven,
but he who does the will of My Father in heaven.
—Matthew 7:21

"Finding God's will" is one of the more mysterious topics in Christianity. It seems most of us don't know what it means. Sometimes finding God's will feels like one of the *National Treasure* movies. Other times it's the punch line of a joke: "She's looking for God's will in her life, so . . . Will, if you're out there, here she is!"

Most of the times in my life when I've tried to determine God's will, it has meant that I need guidance or direction. Feelings of loss, discouragement, and disappointment often drive us to reexamine our lives, and we sense the need for change. Since "The LORD decides what a person will do; no one understands what his life is all about" (Proverbs 20:24 NCV), a wise person will search for what God wants them to do. I have to admit that I've made it harder than it should have been at times. Through trial and error, triumph and failure, I have found two major components to knowing God's will: prayer and the Word of God.

The next chapter in this book is on the subject of prayer, so I will mention it only briefly here. Prayer is one of the two most important steps (in my experience) in discerning God's will. Paul wrote to the Colossian believers and told them he never stopped praying for them so that they would "be filled with the knowledge of His will in all wisdom and spiritual understanding" (Colossians 1:9).

> Prayer is the source of power for growth and perseverance in our spiritual lives . . . Prayer bends our wills to God's will . . . Prayer then is not about getting God to do my bidding, but the shaping and bending of my will until it aligns with His.
>
> —BARBARA HUGHES[54]

One of the greatest insights I have experienced came when I was praying one day, and I realized that Jesus Christ, the Son of God, prayed for His desire, but He submitted to the will of His Father to make the final decision in the matter. On the night before His crucifixion, Jesus went to the garden of Gethsemane to pray. He said, "Father, if it is Your will, take this cup away from Me; nevertheless not My will, but Yours, be done" (Luke 22:42). Jesus prayed a prayer that received the biggest "No" answer in history.

If Jesus was willing to risk praying that prayer, and then leave His fate in the hands of God by saying "not My will, but Yours, be done," then I will follow His example and do the same in my prayers. I will pray for everything I can think of, telling God my biggest hopes, fears, dreams, and disappointments. I will submit to His will by saying "not my will, but Yours, be done," and I will watch Him direct my life. He will open doors that no man can shut, and He will shut other doors that no man can open. I will walk through the open ones, and He will direct my path.

We don't receive what we ask for from God because we ask wrongly for things we want for our own satisfaction (James 4:3). Praying rightly will require giving up our desires and placing ourselves in submission to the will of God. Through prayer, we are transformed to "think God's thoughts after him: to desire the things he desires, to love the things he loves, to will the things he wills."[55]

Another important element in discerning God's will is His Word, the Bible. As we study His Word, learn His attributes, follow His commands, and hear the words of His Son, Jesus Christ, we begin to know God. When we know Him, we can understand what He desires, and this knowledge helps us discern what His will is in the circumstances of life. Barbara Hughes describes the importance of discerning God's will through the Word:

> *The Bible teaches that realizing (or proving) God's will is the result of habitually conforming your thinking and behavior to God's Word over a lifetime . . . The Christian who has ongoing fellowship with the Lord through His Word comes to decisions equipped with a biblically informed way of thinking.*[56]

It is a "biblically informed way of thinking" that helps us know God's will. In the Old Testament (Jeremiah 31:33) and in the New Testament (Hebrews 8:10, 10:16), God says that He will put or write His laws into the hearts and minds of His people. Knowing His Word and laws helps us know His will.

In the classic book *The Christian's Secret to a Happy Life*, Hannah Whitall Smith gives four ways that we are able to discern God's voice:

> How is God's guidance to come to us? . . .

1. The Scriptures. Until you have found and obeyed God's will as revealed in the Bible, you must not ask nor expect a separate, direct, personal revelation. Listening to an inward voice without having first sought out and obeyed the scriptural rules opens ourselves to error . . .

2. Convictions of our higher judgment. Do not rely on isolated texts, but study the principles of the Bible. If you find none to settle your special point of difficulty, seek guidance in the other ways. God will surely voice Himself to you. Remember, "impressions" can come from sources other than the Holy Spirit . . . It is not enough to have a "leading"; we must find the source of that leading and test it by scriptural teachings and our own spiritually enlightened judgment, "common sense" . . .

3. Providential circumstances. If a "leading" is of God, He will go before us and open a way for us to follow. It is never a sign of a divine leading when the Christian insists on battering down doors the Lord has not opened.

4. Inward impressions of the Holy Spirit on our minds. If we feel a "stop in our minds," we must wait until this is removed before acting . . . We must never ignore the voice of our inward impressions . . .

Take your perplexities to the Lord and ask Him to make plain His will for you.

Promise to obey and believe implicitly He is guiding you.[57]

Hannah Smith wrote her book in 1883. It is a testament to the truth of her words that her wisdom still holds true today. It is interesting to me that she used the word *perplexities*. I have a note in my journal quoting *The Circle Maker* by Mark Batterson that asks, "Are you willing to be perplexed? If you are, then God can and will amaze you!"[58] Just to make sure that I knew the meaning of the word *perplexed*, I looked it up. One who is perplexed is filled with uncertainty. Synonyms include *puzzled, baffled, confounded, bewildered, flustered*, and *put out*.

I found *The Circle Maker* quote less than seven weeks after getting fired, so my family was feeling all of the definitions of *perplexed*. That day, I wrote this prayer: "God, we are perplexed—we have been since January 7. We may not having willingly chosen to be perplexed, but we are. And now we can say that we are glad to have been perplexed. Now let's be amazed!"

I want to be amazed because *amazed* means "filled with wonder, astounded." The synonyms are *surprised, astonished, bowled over, rocked, stunned,* and *blown away*. As of today, it has been seventeen months since I prayed that prayer, and I can say with certainty that we have been amazed. We have been amazed at the outpouring of love and support from our family, church, friends, and community. We have been amazed at the Lord's leading, the guidance of His Word, and the comfort of the Holy Spirit. We have been amazed by His provision. We have been amazed at the changes He has made in our hearts. We are different people than we were before being perplexed. We are amazed!

> Show me Your ways, O Lord; teach me Your paths. Lead me in Your truth and teach me, for You are the God of my salvation; on You I wait all the day.
>
> —PSALM 25:4–5

I wish I could write today and tell you we have a clear pathway that we are walking and that we know exactly where we are headed. But I can't because we don't. Every day is a new challenge. Every day is a new opportunity to ask God to help us. Every day is another chance to walk through open doors or be hit in the face by the ones that are closing. And here's the thing . . . we never know which type of day it will be. Today we may be perplexed, but maybe we'll be amazed. That's what makes God's will so exciting!

Prayer

Dear Father, take this day's life into Thine own keeping. Control all my thoughts and feelings. Direct all my energies. Instruct my mind. Sustain my will. Take my hands and make them skillful to serve

Thee. Take my feet and make them swift to do Thy bidding. Take my eyes and keep them fixed upon Thine everlasting beauty.

—John Baillie[59]

And lovingly, I pray to thee, O God, by Your goodness give me Yourself, for You are enough for me.

—Julian of Norwich

I will do anything that Your kingdom requires of me. Wherever you want me to be, I'll go. Whatever the circumstances, I'm willing to follow. If You want to meet a need through my life, I am Your servant; and I will do whatever is required.

—Richard Blackaby[60]

…

God, I am trying wholeheartedly to trust in You, and I am certainly not depending on my own understanding. I am seeking Your will, direction, and guidance about what You want me to do. Please show me which path to take. God, do not wait. Holy Spirit, I need Your help. In Jesus' name.

The Promises of God

And Jabez called on the God of Israel saying, "Oh, that You would bless me indeed, and enlarge my territory, that Your hand would be with me, and that You would keep me from evil, that I may not cause pain!" So God granted him what he requested.

1 Chronicles 4:10

I will not leave you comfortless: I will come to you.

John 14:18 KJV

Call to Me, and I will answer you, and show you great and mighty things, which you do not know.

Jeremiah 33:3

Trust in the LORD with all your heart, and lean not on your own understanding; in all your ways acknowledge Him, and He shall direct your paths.

Proverbs 3:5–6

I will bring the blind by a way they did not know; I will lead them in paths they have not known. I will make darkness light before them, and crooked places straight. These things I will do for them, and not forsake them.

Isaiah 42:16

May He grant you according to your heart's desire, and fulfill all your purpose.

Psalm 20:4

Part Four

ASK

"Kimmy, you've got the gimmes."
—My mom to me,
from about ages 3–18!

We ask a lot of people for a lot of things, and yet, we often fail to ask God for His help and intervention in our lives. By not asking, we miss the opportunity to see and experience the supernatural intervention of God in daily life. Does God do something differently because we ask Him to? I don't know, but I do know that if we haven't asked God for help or provision or what we need, and it is provided, we don't recognize it as having been provided by God to us. We assume it just happened, and that assumption denies God glory He should have received.

I hoped so strongly to become more aware of God's working in my life that I wrote a prayer to pray every day. The prayer says, "God, please do something today to show me that You're working on my behalf. Make me see and realize what You do!"

We are hesitant to ask God for what we need because we don't want to be selfish or greedy, but God wants us to ask. James 4:2 says that "you do not have because you do not ask." It is of utmost importance that we ask God for our dreams, hopes, desires, and needs from a pure heart and godly motives; but not asking God for anything because we are afraid we might ask for the wrong thing accomplishes nothing.

So ask . . . and keep asking. God knows we are human beings with finite comprehension of the world around us. We cannot know everything we need. We certainly cannot know everything God knows, so He listens patiently to our requests and helps us determine His will and direction in our lives through our prayers.

We should not be afraid to lay out our biggest hopes and desires in our prayers. I am praying for some things that I wouldn't tell anyone about except God and my husband, because anyone else would think I am nuts! I'm finding that as I pray my seemingly impossible prayers, my faith is strengthened because I hear myself verbalizing my deepest desires; and I start remembering prayers that God has answered in the past. If He has been faithful to answer in the past, I know He will be faithful to answer again in the future. He may not answer in the way that I thought He would or the way that I wanted, but He will answer.

So bombard God with your requests. King David did. He said, "I will call to God for help, and the Lord will save me. Morning, noon, and night I am troubled and upset, but he will listen to me" (Psalm 55:16–17 NCV); "Hear my prayer, God;

listen to what I say" (Psalm 54:2 NCV); "God, listen to my prayer and do not ignore my cry for help. Pay attention to me and answer me" (Psalm 55:1–2 NCV). Don't stop praying until your rebellious child comes home. Don't stop praying until you have a financial breakthrough. Don't stop praying until your marriage is repaired. Don't stop praying until your body is healed. Don't stop praying until you know God's will in the situation. Whatever else you do, don't stop praying. I guess I still have "the gimmes." Now I'm just asking Someone else for what I need!

Chapter 11

Pray

*The determined fixing of our will upon God,
and pressing toward Him steadily and without deflection:
this is the very center and the art of prayer.*
—Evelyn Underhill[61]

• • •

*Hear me, O LORD, for Your lovingkindness is good;
turn to me according to the multitude of Your tender mercies.
And do not hide Your face from Your servant, for I am in trouble; hear me speedily. Draw near to my soul, and redeem it;
deliver me because of my enemies.*
—Psalm 69:16–18

The single greatest step to take in moving from hurt to hope is prayer. I have so many notes on the subject of prayer that this chapter could become an entire book. Most of these notes have been written during my search for encouragement, help, and comfort in the last eighteen months. Several books have been especially helpful and have changed my prayer life, and

I highly recommend them: Stormie Omartian's *The Power of a Praying Woman*, *The Power of a Praying Wife,* and the *Power of a Praying Parent*; *Celebration of Discipline* by Richard Foster; *The Circle Maker* by Mark Batterson; *A Diary of Private Prayer* by John Baillie; *Mighty Prevailing Prayer* by Wesley L. Duewel; and *Prayer* by George Buttrick.

Before studying and practicing these works, I never thought I knew how to pray. Growing up in church, I was told that you just talk to God like you talk to a friend. I have passed this advice on to people myself, but the more I study prayer, and the lives of people who know how to pray, there is much more to prayer than just talking.

It was during my first class in biblical counseling studies, Spiritual Formation for Women, that I started to study prayer. I was introduced to the devotional masters, writers throughout history who have spent their lives learning how to study and pray in an attempt to know God. I studied inspired writers and thinkers such as St. John of the Cross, Evelyn Underhill, St. Augustine, C.S. Lewis, Francis de Sales, Julian of Norwich, and Henri J.M. Nouwen (to name a few) who have written some of the most beautiful, profound, thought-provoking literature ever penned.

One of my favorite devotional masters is Brother Lawrence, an uneducated Carmelite brother (a worker in a monastery who was not a priest) in Paris in the 1600s who never wrote a book. However, the book containing his letters, *The Practice of the Presence of God*, has changed the lives, particularly the prayer lives, of many people, myself included. Brother Lawrence tried to live in constant communication with God. He wrote, "I make it my business to rest in His holy presence, which I keep myself in by a habitual, silent, and secret conversation with God."[62] This must have been difficult because Brother Lawrence was assigned to kitchen duty at the monastery, which he admitted he did not enjoy. He used his dislike of his duties as his gift in service to God. He turned drudgery into devotion, and he learned how to pray in the midst of the kitchen noise. He wrote, "The time of business does not differ from the time of prayer, and in the noise and clatter of my kitchen, while several persons are at the same time calling for different things, I possess God in as great tranquility as if I were on my knees at the Blessed Sacrament."[63] Brother Lawrence's reputation as a man of serenity, prayer, and devotion to God became so well-known that the pope came to visit him to find the secret to his serenity.

Brother Lawrence's description of the kitchen he worked in sounds similar to our modern lives. We live in the noise and clatter of the world, but we need to come away from it in order to learn how to pray, listen, and know God.

> I have just returned from a walk alone, a walk so wonderful that I feel like reducing it to a universal rule, that all people ought to take a walk every evening all alone where they can talk aloud without being heard by anyone, and that during this entire walk they all ought to talk with God, allowing him to use their tongues to talk back—and letting God do most of the talking.
>
> —FRANK LAUBACH, *Letters by a Modern Mystic*[64]

So how can we come away from our noisy world and hear God? Honestly, it is hard, but it can be done. Brother Lawrence could do it in the middle of the clatter, but most of us cannot. We need solitude—being alone. No mobile device. No music. No book. Just you and God. Music and books are great resources for encouragement and knowledge, but prayer solitude requires no distractions to listening to the voice of God. Prayer is communication, and communication requires both talking and listening. It usually requires a special time and place of solitude.

My place of solitude is my home office, and the time is early in the morning before anyone else in my home is awake. I also benefit from the solitude and prayer of walking. I can walk two miles in my neighborhood early in the morning and usually never see another person. These times of solitude have been essential to my spiritual health. When I'm walking, I'm praying. Sometimes I'm begging God for help. Sometimes I'm thanking Him for His help and blessing. Sometimes I'm asking for wisdom.

Listening happens naturally when I'm away from the noise of life, where I can be quiet and listen to that "still small voice" (1 Kings 19:11–13). It is awesome to realize that the Holy Spirit of the God of the universe can whisper to us if we have a receptive, quiet spirit.

There are times of listening prayer in quiet and solitude, and there are also times of prayer when we bring our requests to the Lord. We must learn to pray thoroughly, specifically, and powerfully.

PRAYING THOROUGHLY

There are several aspects to prayer that can be confusing or overwhelming if we do not have a specific plan to pray thoroughly. I found a helpful how-to list when I read a synopsis of an exhaustive book on prayer written in 1942 by George Buttrick—the pastor of Madison Avenue Presbyterian Church in New York City. This book, titled *Prayer*, is considered one of the most comprehensive works ever written on prayer.

Reverend Buttrick suggests the following steps to prayer:

1. **Silent self-preparation.** Sit silently, ready to speak to and hear from God.
2. **Act of Faith.** Remind yourself of the benefits of faith, such as "whatever we ask in the nature of Christ is ours," and "all things whatever you ask in prayer, believing, you will receive."
3. **Thanksgiving.** Call to mind the joys of the journey. Be specific and write down the blessings of one day.
4. **Confession.** Confess and renounce sin. Confession should be ruthless, not an excuse.
5. **Contrition.** Determine to make wise restitution and accept God's pardon through Jesus Christ.
6. **Intercession.** Start by praying the Lord's Prayer, then move to prayer for another. Make a chart of intercession in order to specifically name those for whom you will pray.

7. **Petition.** This is lifting your needs before Eternal Eyes. Always conclude with the prayer that Jesus prayed in the Garden before His crucifixion: "Nevertheless, not my will, but Yours be done."

8. **Adoration.** Meditate on who God is and what He has done in giving His Son Jesus as the remission for sin. End by praying in the name of Jesus.[65]

I have practiced these steps in prayer for over five years, and I have found them to be an excellent tool. They help in praying thoroughly.

PRAYING SPECIFICALLY

The greatest work that I have read in praying specifically is *The Circle Maker*. I have read the book, reread it, filled a notebook with notes and quotes from it, and studied it in a Bible study. I pull it out almost weekly for inspiration to pray.

> God's name, God's kingdom, God's will must be the primary object of Christian prayer.
>
> —DIETRICH BONHOEFFER[69]

From the first day I started reading the book, I got a notebook, a water glass, and a pen, and I started drawing prayer circles. The first prayer circle I drew asks for "God's will and direction to be revealed and presented to us." Inside each prayer circle is a specific prayer. If you specify your prayers, you will be able to pray specifically and get a specific answer. *The Circle Maker* taught me to Dream Big, Pray Hard, and Think Long.

PRAYING POWERFULLY

Mighty Prevailing Prayer by Wesley Duewel teaches how to pray powerfully. It drives home the importance of persevering in prayer through difficult circumstances. Duewel writes, "Prayer is so vital to all of Christian life and to the advancement of Christ's kingdom that He desires all of us to be mighty in prayer, experienced in getting prayer answers, and undismayed by the most complex or longstanding needs."[66]

If you are reading this book because you've gone through something that has hurt you, or if you are looking for help, relief, and answers, you must be mighty in prevailing prayer because "we must prevail in prayer for situations where God's will is being thwarted and where Satan is delaying and blocking Christ's cause. . . . Prevailing prayer is intercession intensified—intercession until the answer is received."[67]

Praying powerfully may involve fasting. It may require giving up some form of entertainment so there is time to pray powerfully. It may mean "holding on to God," as the old-timers used to say. Prevailing prayer requires faith to believe that God will do what He said He would do, even when the circumstances say otherwise.

Prayer will often bring about a change in circumstances, but it will always bring about a change in you. Prayer forces you to let go of your will and let God have His will be accomplished through you and in you. In *Celebration of Discipline*, Richard Foster writes, "To pray is to change. If we are unwilling to change, we will abandon prayer as a noticeable characteristic in our lives. The closer we come to the heartbeat of God the more we see our need and the more we desire to be conformed to Christ."[68]

Gary's grandparents, Glenn and Elsie Shover, were the prayer warriors of his family. They prayed for everyone and everything. They were married for sixty-four years before Nanny Elsie passed away; and at the time of her death, there were two-hundred fifty names on their prayer list for whom they spent hours praying daily. In 1995, they gave Gary and me the book *Mighty Prevailing Prayer*. Nanny wrote a note to us in the front of the book that said, "Keep this book always. It will teach you how to pray. It has sure helped me. It will even benefit your children as they grow in the Lord. You can refer back to it to help and encourage you, for we are human and we forget."

Nanny Elsie was (and still is) an inspiration to her family. She and Popaw Glenn selflessly gave of their time to pray for others, and lives have been eternally transformed because of their praying thoroughly, specifically, and powerfully. My prayer is that we all learn to do the same.

Prayer

My God, my God, why have you rejected me? You seem far away from saving me, far from the words of my groaning. My God, I call to You during the day, but You do not answer. I call at night; I am not silent. So don't be far away from me. Now trouble is near and there is no one to help. My strength is gone

. . . my heart is like wax. But Lord, don't be far away. You are my strength; hurry to help me. You do not ignore those in trouble (Psalm 22).

Lord, You are my strength and shield. I trust You and You help me. I am very happy, and I praise You with my song (Psalm 28:7).

Lord, Your Word promises that whoever loves You will be saved, protected, and answered (Psalm 91:14–16). I need those promises to be a reality in my life. I am calling to You knowing that You will answer me. You will be with me when I am in trouble. You will rescue me, honor me, and give me a long, full life. Then I will see how You have saved! I thank You for all of these promises and blessings. In the name of Jesus, amen.

The Promises of God

Every morning you'll hear me at it again. Every morning I lay out the pieces of my life on your altar and watch for fire to descend.

Psalm 5:3 MSG

I will call upon the LORD, who is worthy to be praised; so shall I be saved from my enemies.

2 Samuel 22:4

Call to me and I will answer you and tell you great and unsearchable things you do not know.

Jeremiah 33:3 NIV

But giving thanks is a sacrifice that truly honors me. If you keep to my path, I will reveal to you the salvation of God.

Psalm 50:23 NLT

Also, I tell you that if two of you on earth agree about something and pray for it, it will be done for you by my Father in heaven. This is true because if two or three people come together in my name, I am there with them.

Matthew 18:19–20 NCV

Chapter 12

Be Wise

Wisdom is the principal thing; therefore get wisdom.
And in all your getting, get understanding.
—*Proverbs 4:7*

When I was Miss Florida, I was asked by a Christian college to come and sing at a special chapel service that was honoring women in ministry. I accepted the invitation and was happy to be a part of the service.

The morning of the event, I prepared as usual for an appearance as Miss Florida. I put on my makeup, fixed my hair, wore an appropriate dress, and practiced the song that I would sing. I arrived at the college, had a sound check, and waited for the service to begin.

I was introduced to sing shortly after the service started. I sang, sat back down with the other ladies on the platform, and mentally congratulated myself on a job well done. The speaker that morning was a missionary. She was about eighty years old, and cute as can be. She wore a conservative navy-blue suit with orthopedic shoes. Her gray hair was combed into the perfect bun. She shuffled slowly to the podium and began to tell her story.

She had gone to Africa with her husband forty years earlier to begin their missionary work. They lived in a native village where she taught the local women how to cook and clean in a sanitary manner that was not practiced at that time. She delivered babies, and she taught children to read. Twenty years after arriving in Africa, her husband passed away, but she stayed there another twenty years alone to continue their work. Many natives accepted Jesus Christ as their Savior thanks to the selfless dedication of this little missionary lady.

The longer this precious woman spoke, the more embarrassed I became. I was sitting behind her on the platform, and I felt as if a giant spotlight were shining on me. I could almost hear a voice announcing, "This chick has no right to be on the same stage with this missionary. Just ask her. She knows why."

And I did know why. I had been more concerned that day about what I would wear and how I would fix my hair than I had been about any type of ministry that might occur. I had prepared to be Miss Florida, but I had not prepared to be convicted by an eighty-year-old woman.

That morning was a turning point in my life. I knew that if I wanted to become a wise, godly woman—which I do—I had to make some changes. For the first time in my life, I think I really experienced the fear of God. Not the type of fear that results in stark terror, but the kind that makes you think about how insignificant we are in comparison to His majesty. The kind of fear that makes you realize that you are not "all that," but that

He is! The kind that makes you awestruck by His power and might. It is a submissive reverence, an understanding of God that inspires us to become His obedient servants.

The alternative to fearing God and allowing Him to rule our lives is to do what *The Message* version of Proverbs 1:7 says: "thumb [our] noses at such wisdom and learning." We can attempt to run our own lives as we see fit. We can try to be wise and learn apart from God, and we may possibly reach a point where we begin to think we can live without Him. We might even feel we have reached the point intellectually where we don't need to bow to Him, and we can say that there is no God; but only a fool says in his heart there is no God (Psalm 14:1).

> Help me to walk uprightly, righteously, and obediently to Your commands.
>
> —STORMIE OMARTIAN[70]

Eventually we all face problems and situations we cannot overcome. We end up broken and battered. That's why we need God. That's why we need a Savior. We all try to be self-sufficient heroes, but end up feeling like zeroes more often. The scars we collect can go deep. And we can't fix ourselves. We try drugs, alcohol, relationships, therapy, money, and anything else we think will dull the pain, but we always end up being scarred zeroes, not genuine heroes. But we will always *need* a hero. That hero can only be God Almighty because "There is no one like you, Lord, and there is no God but you" (1 Chronicles 17:20 NIV). "There is no one holy like the Lord; there is no one besides you; there is no Rock like our God" (1 Samuel 2:2 NIV).[71]

"With Him are wisdom and strength, He has counsel and understanding" (Job 12:13). In order to become wise, you must study God and His Word. It is impossible to have true wisdom without fearing God and His commandments (Psalm 111:10). Biblical wisdom exists as practical, instructional skills for everyday living, and as guidance toward moral behavior. Wisdom means living skillfully, but it is impossible to live skillfully in God's way without a determined effort. "Apply your heart to instruction, and your ears to words of knowledge" (Proverbs 23:12). It will take study, effort, and listening to become wise.

Wisdom is the power to see, and the inclination to choose, the best and highest goal, together with the surest means of attaining it. Wisdom is, in fact, the practical side of moral goodness. As such, it is found in its fullness only in God. He alone is naturally and entirely and invariable wise.

—J.I. PACKER[72]

Remember the Bible story of a young Samuel who was spoken to three times in one night by the voice of God, but he didn't recognize it? It took the wisdom of the older prophet, Eli, to understand what was happening and advise Samuel what to do. Eli wisely told Samuel to say, "Speak, LORD. I am your servant and I am listening" (1 Samuel 3:9 NCV). Then Samuel heard and responded to the voice of the Lord.

For the Christian, living skillfully and wisely is accomplished through the power of the Holy Spirit. The Holy Spirit is given many titles in Scripture. He is Guide (John 16:13), Comforter

(John 14:16), Teacher (John 14:26), Power (Acts 1:8), Counselor (John 14:26), Advocate (Romans 8:16), Helper (John 14:6), and Truth (John 15:26). The Spirit of the Lord gives "wisdom and understanding, the Spirit of counsel and might, the Spirit of knowledge and of the fear of the LORD" (Isaiah 11:2).

At this point in my journey from hurt to hope, I need wisdom from "the Spirit of counsel and might." I was doing a Bible study recently, and a phrase was particularly interesting. It said, "Paul felt compelled by the Spirit" (Acts 19:21 NLT). I have some major decisions to make concerning what direction to pursue professionally. I need to be wise, and I want to feel "compelled by the Spirit" to the right course. I looked up several translations of the same phrase to get a better understanding of the Scripture's intent. *The Message* says, "Paul decided"; the King James Version reads, "Paul purposed in the spirit." A note in the *Dake Annotated Reference Bible* says "[Paul] firmly resolved in his spirit or mind."[73] Paul felt compelled, decided, purposed, and firmly resolved.

That is the type of Holy Spirit–inspired wisdom that I need. It's what you need. It's what we all need as we seek direction and guidance on a journey from hurt to hope. In a related passage, the *Dake* Bible goes on to say that there are two kinds of wisdom: words of man's wisdom, and words of Holy Ghost wisdom. The spiritual "man is living under the control of the Holy Spirit and minds the things of the Spirit. He has the mind of Christ and discerns and esteems spiritual things above the sensual. He is a new creature and resurrected from death in trespasses and sins. The lower animal passions have been crucified and put off."[74]

There is that biblical counseling principle of "putting off" and "putting on" again. We must put off the old man or woman with the old ways of thinking, acting, and reacting, and put on the new man or woman with the new, Christlike, Spirit-inspired, and Spirit-led way of thinking, acting, and reacting. This is true wisdom: to fear God, obey His commands, and follow His ways.

The wisdom of man is futile. The book of Ecclesiastes makes this point and is fairly depressing to an optimist. One of the book's points is that trying to become wise simply for the sake of wisdom is useless. Yet God commands His children to live wisely. We desire to live wisely and follow God's commands because we are awestruck at His majesty, and we rely on the power of the Holy Spirit to help us.

> You said in Your Word that You store up sound wisdom for the upright.
>
> —PROVERBS 2:7

The results and rewards of a Spirit-led life of wisdom are talked about consistently in the Bible. The contrast between a life of wisdom and righteousness and a life of folly, foolishness, and wickedness is the overarching theme of the book of Proverbs. Take a quick look:

"The fear of the LORD is the beginning of knowledge, but fools despise wisdom and instruction" (1:7).

"For the turning away of the simple will slay them, and the complacency of fools will destroy them; but whoever listens to me will dwell safely, and will be secure, without fear of evil" (1:32–33).

"The curse of the LORD is on the house of the wicked, but

He blesses the home of the just. Surely He scorns the scornful, but gives grace to the humble. The wise shall inherit glory, but shame shall be the legacy of fools" (3:33–35).

"But the path of the just is like the shining sun, that shines ever brighter unto the perfect day. The way of the wicked is like darkness; they do not know what makes them stumble" (4:18–19).

"A wise son makes a glad father, but a foolish son is the grief of his mother. Treasures of wickedness profit nothing, but righteousness delivers from death. The LORD will not allow the righteous soul to famish, but He casts away the desire of the wicked" (10:1–3).

"Blessings are on the head of the righteous, but violence covers the mouth of the wicked. The memory of the righteous is blessed, but the name of the wicked will rot. The wise in heart will receive commands, but a prating fool will fall. He who walks with integrity walks securely, but he who perverts his ways will become known" (10:6–9).

These are just a few of the many Scriptures in Proverbs that draw great distinctions between wise and foolish living. A wise, righteous life is rewarded. This is not to claim that wisdom and righteousness protect from all trouble. They don't. We live in a fallen world, and as fallible, imperfect human beings we will never be free from the effects of sin. However, the blessings of obedience, wisdom, and righteousness outweigh the burden and sorrow of foolishness and evil. A few of the blessings of wisdom are:

Abundant life—"The thief does not come except to steal, and to kill, and to destroy. I have come that they may have life, and that they may have it more abundantly" (John 10:10).

Peace—"Peace I leave with you, My peace I give to you; not as the world gives do I give to you. Let not your heart be troubled, neither let it be afraid" (John 14:27).

Guidance—"I have taught you in the way of wisdom; I have led you in right paths. When you walk, your steps will not be hindered, and when you run, you will not stumble" (Proverbs 4:11–12).

Deliverance—"He who trusts in his own heart is a fool, but whoever walks wisely will be delivered" (Proverbs 28:26).

Eternal life—"So when this corruptible has put on incorruption, and this mortal has put on immortality, then shall be brought to pass the saying that is written: 'Death is swallowed up in victory'" (1 Corinthians 15:54).

Thirty years ago I determined to become wise. I do not feel that I have arrived, but my quest has brought blessing and joy to my life. It has helped sustain me on the journey from hurt to hope. It can do the same for you.

Prayer

Lord, It is a desire of my heart to become wise. I pray that Your Holy Spirit would fill me with wisdom and teach me to live skillfully according to Your commands.

The Promises of God

Happy is the man who finds wisdom, and the man who gains understanding; for her proceeds are better than the profits of silver, and her gain than fine gold.

Proverbs 3:13–14

The LORD will work out his plans for my life—for your faithful love, O LORD, endures forever. Don't abandon me, for you made me.

Psalm 138:8 NLT

When wisdom enters your heart, and knowledge is pleasant to your soul, discretion will preserve you; understanding will keep you, to deliver you from the way of evil, from the man who speaks perverse things, from those who leave the paths of uprightness.

Proverbs 2:10–13

For to be carnally minded is death, but to be spiritually minded is life and peace.

Romans 8:6

There is no wisdom, understanding, or advice that can succeed against the LORD.

Proverbs 21:30 NCV

My child, if you are wise, then I will be happy.

Proverbs 23:15 NCV

Chapter 13

Wait–Then Run!

But those who wait on the Lord shall renew their strength;
they shall mount up with wings like eagles, they shall run
and not be weary, they shall walk and not faint.
—*Isaiah 40:31*

Six months into my journey from hurt to hope I wrote this:

Our lives have been completely changed. Right now,
Gary and our boys are mowing lawns for income.
We've had a couple of invitations to sing in churches,
but not enough invitations to believe that that's the
avenue of ministry that God has planned for us. You
would think that my former career in Contempo-
rary Christian Music would open doors somewhere,
wouldn't you? But I have heard "No" a lot more than
I've heard "Yes" lately. In other words, I'm losing heart.

Gary and I have been on a Daniel Fast for the past
six days. We decided last week that we needed more
ammunition in the prayer arsenal, so we committed

to prayer and fasting for ten days. We have two spe-cific requests that we are praying for during the fast, and six days into it . . . nothing. This morning I wrote a prayer that told God my faith is faltering. I told Him I'm losing heart, but I will keep praying, believing, and struggling because I know that He will come through and then we will experience the supernatural break-through that we need.

What else can I do? We've been in this wilderness of uncertainty, disappointment, and discouragement for six months. Somehow it feels as if it's been longer. I keep reading the encouraging words that a lady spoke to Gary and me recently. She said, "Because you've been faithful in the little things, God is blessing you with a double portion. This feels like a setback, but it's actually a promotion!" She's right about it feeling like a setback. It feels like a setback, a demotion, and a bad dream. We need direction. We need guidance and some answers. There's an old saying, "Pray like it depends on God, and work like it depends on you." We have been doing these things. Every day has been a day of praying. So much so that I'm beginning to think that God is getting sick of hearing the same requests from me, day in and day out. Something is going to occur that will make everything that I've written so far make sense. I want to say like King David said, "I will praise you, Lord, with all my heart. I will tell all the miracles you have done" (Psalm 9:1 NCV).

Another year has gone by, and now the question is: "Am I going to praise Him *until* I see the miracles?" or "Am I going to praise Him if I *never* see any miracles?" And "Am I going to praise Him if He answers my prayers with miracles that are not what I thought I wanted and needed?" The question is not whether or not He will perform miracles. David said he would tell all the miracles God had done. God does perform miracles. We just take them for granted.

It's a miracle that the sun came up this morning. It's a miracle that the earth hasn't veered a little bit off course, gotten too close to the sun, and burned up the entire planet. It's a miracle that a complete stranger, Danielle, saw a nineteen-year-old video of mine online, contacted me, drove two and a half hours to hang out at church with me, now believes there is a God, has asked Jesus to become her Lord and Savior, and has become one of the first patients in a new cancer treatment program that has given her the ability to fight the death sentence that she had been given. Maybe it's a miracle that I'm writing a book to try to help someone else when I could have allowed disappointment, betrayal, and hurt to ruin me.

I can be willful when I need to be. I can be stubborn. I can set my mind on something and not be turned back, and now is the time to be willful, stubborn, and set. I will to be faithful, standing strong during this time of trouble. You can do the same. Determine by faith that with God's help, you will be strong. Paul wrote, "So do not lose the courage you had in the past, which has a great reward. You must hold on, so you can do what God wants and receive what he has promised. For in a very short time, 'The One who is coming will come and will not be delayed. Those who are right with me will live by faith. But if they turn back with fear, I will not be pleased with them.' But we are not those who turn back and are lost. We are people who have faith and are saved" (Hebrews 10:35–39 NCV). So we must live by trusting in God and not turn back in fear. How do we do that? By standing on the promises that God has given us concerning His trustworthiness.

Ready. Set. Wait. These words seem to be my course. I've been ready for something amazing to happen to change our circumstances. I've set about working to do my part to help something amazing happen. And now I pray and work and wait. I don't like waiting. By nature, I am not a patient person; that's probably the reason God makes me wait. He's trying to teach me something important through waiting. He certainly seems to use waiting a lot as a means of spiritual growth.

Scripture is full of references to waiting, such as Isaiah 40:31: "But those who wait on the LORD shall renew their strength; they shall mount up with wings like eagles, they shall run and not be weary, they shall walk and not faint."

See also Psalm 40:1–3 (NCV): "I waited patiently for the LORD. He turned to me and heard my cry. He lifted me out of the pit of destruction, out of the sticky mud. He stood me on a rock and made my feet steady. He put a new song in my mouth, a song of praise to our God. Many people will see this and worship him. Then they will trust the LORD."

So if I wait for Him, He hears me when I cry. He lifts me out of my pit and puts me somewhere with a firm foundation.

He gives me something new to say and sing about that praises Him; then others will see what He has done for me, and it will strengthen their faith and trust in God.

So I'll wait! And here's the thing: I can only wait for one day. Today. I can only wait today because today is the only day that I have. Perhaps I will wait again tomorrow, but maybe I won't! Maybe something incredible happens tomorrow that makes waiting today worthwhile.

While I wait today, I will attempt to seek first His kingdom and His righteousness; to love my enemies; to fear not; and to ask Him to provide what He knows I need. I'll keep praying and working and trying not to worry because Matthew 6:34 (NCV) says, "So don't worry about tomorrow, because tomorrow will have its own worries. Each day has enough trouble of its own." I'll keep waiting.

There will be a day when the waiting is over. It could be today, tomorrow, or a day next year, or ten years from now. I don't know when I will stop waiting. I don't know when you will stop waiting, but one day you will. That will be the day to start running!

I love something that Stormie Omartian wrote. She said, "When God chooses to move, He often makes quick work of it." How true. Often it seems as though we wait around for something to happen, and then all of a sudden, the waiting is over and we have to run just to keep up!

If you want and need inspiration to run, watch the scene in the movie *Secretariat* where Secretariat wins the Belmont Stakes to take the Triple Crown in 1973. You can see the actual event online too. It's amazing to watch. The Belmont track is the longest track of the Triple Crown series, and none of the horses in the race has ever run a race this long competitively before. The horses come out of the gate, and Secretariat takes the lead.

Although he is favored to win, and though Secretariat is in the lead at the first turn, the announcers are proclaiming his demise. They do not believe he can keep such a pace to win the race. Yet Secretariat is in the lead at the second turn. On the backstretch straightaway something unbelievable happens.

> If you want to experience a supernatural breakthrough, you have to pray through. But as you get closer to the breakthrough, it often feels like you're about to lose control, about to fall apart. That is when you need to press in and pray through. If you allow them to, your disappointments will create drag. But if you pray through, God will come through and you'll experience a supernatural breakthrough.
>
> —MARK BATTERSON[75]

Secretariat begins pulling away from the rest of the horses. At a time in the race when a horse should be tiring and beginning to slow down, Secretariat is picking up speed.

Now the announcers are screaming that they can't believe their eyes. How is this happening? It's impossible. By the final turn, Secretariat has left the rest of the horses far behind. In a field where a race is usually won by less than one or two lengths, Secretariat has no challenger. The question continues to be: "Can he keep up the pace?" With a quarter mile to go, Secretariat runs even faster. When he crosses the finish line, he is thirty-one lengths ahead of his nearest competitor. His race time is still the fastest finish at the Belmont Stakes and in the history of horse racing.

It's as if God said, "I've created this beautiful animal. Now, watch what he can do." He touched him for an instant, and a horse amazed us all. I may be the only person in the world who cried my eyes out at the result of a horse race, but I saw God's touch. I saw God's anointing. I saw God's glory. For an instant, no one could deny that something supernatural had occurred. I'm speculating now, but if God did that for a horse, doesn't it seem possible that He would do it for His child? For you? For me? I believe with all of my heart that He will!

The place between "waiting" and "running" is the hard part. Waiting is mundane. Waiting is boring. Waiting means doing the same thing today that you did yesterday. It's cooking, cleaning, working, buying, selling, driving, talking, mowing, mothering, fathering, and a hundred other regular, everyday tasks.

I've come to the place where *I don't know what else to do.* I'm beyond trusting in my own abilities. I'm at the end of my self-sufficient rope . . . waiting. This is probably right where God wanted me to be all along. Waiting is preparation and training. It's spiritual exercise. It is a training period for the big race. It's preparing you and me to run the race with endurance (Hebrews 12:1). Waiting should be developing the things important to God in our lives. Things like love, joy, peace, patience, kindness, goodness, faithfulness, gentleness, and self-control (Galatians 5:22–23). Waiting, along with testing, refines our character.

One day, the buzzer will sound, the chute will open, and you will be off and running. The preparation, training, and waiting will be put to use as you run through whatever doors God has chosen to open. Run like Secretariat. Run and amaze people. Run until people see God's touch. Run until they see His anointing. Run until they see His *glory*!

Prayer

"Show me where to walk, for I give myself to you" (Psalm 143:8 NLT). "Point out the road I must travel; I'm all ears, all eyes before you" (MSG). "Show me what I should do, because my prayers go up to You" (NCV). "Cause me to know the way wherein I should walk; for I lift up my soul unto thee" (KJV).

The Promises of God

Wait for the LORD's help. Be strong and brave, and wait for the LORD's help.

Psalm 27:14 NCV

Wait for the LORD's help and follow him. He will honor you and give you the land, and you will see the wicked sent away.

Psalm 37:34 NCV

Trust in the LORD with all your heart, and lean not on your own understanding; in all your ways acknowledge Him, and He shall direct your paths.

Proverbs 3:5–6

Joyful are those who have the God of Israel as their helper, whose hope is in the LORD their God. He made heaven and earth, the sea, and everything in them. He keeps every promise forever.

Psalm 146:5–6 NLT

With God's power working in us, God can do much, much more than anything we can ask or imagine.

Ephesians 3:20 NCV

But he said to me, "My grace is enough for you. When you are weak, my power is made perfect in you."

2 Corinthians 12:9 NCV

I can do all things through Christ who strengthens me.

Philippians 4:13

God began doing a good work in you, and I am sure he will continue it until it is finished when Jesus Christ comes again.

Philippians 1:6 NCV

I have fought the good fight, I have finished the race, I have kept the faith.

2 Timothy 4:7 NCV

When you pass through the waters, I will be with you. When you cross rivers, you will not drown. When you walk through fire, you will not be burned, nor will the flames hurt you. This is because I, the LORD, am your God, the Holy One of Israel, your Savior.

Isaiah 43:2–3

Epilogue

Stand at the crossroads and look;
ask for the ancient paths, ask where the good way is,
and walk in it, and you will find rest for your souls.
—Jeremiah 6:16 NIV

As you've been reading this book, you have taken the journey and have the tools that can lead you from hurt to hope. I pray that the directives that were given to me have helped you. The four major principles, *Seek First the Kingdom*, *Love Your Enemies*, *Fear Not*, and *Ask* have provided a solid foundation for the journey. The twelve chapters can move us further from hurt and closer to hope and healing. You have sought "the good way" as Jeremiah 6:16 says, and what has been presented are the tried-and-true ways that godly men and women throughout the history of Christianity have walked from faith to faith.

This journey, however, cannot be taken alone. You must take this journey with your hand firmly placed within the hand of Jesus Christ, the Savior. We need Him to save us from sin and the painful effects of living in a fallen world. We need His Spirit to teach us to think correctly and not fall prey to a victim mentality after being wounded. We need to trust Him, rather than risking our sanity by asking "Why?" We are fallible human beings, but He is God Almighty. We cannot comprehend His ways, and we cannot understand His plan. But we can stand up, brush ourselves off, and *believe that He has one.* That may be the single most important step of all!

For the good that comes in your life from the reading of this book, I say, "Praise and glory and wisdom and thanks and honor and power and strength be to our God for ever and ever. Amen!" (Revelation 7:12 NIV).

The LORD bless you and keep you; the LORD make His face shine upon you, and be gracious to you; the LORD lift up His countenance upon you, and give you peace.

—Numbers 6:24–26

And now I entrust you to God and the message of his grace that is able to build you up and give you an inheritance with all those he has set apart for himself.

—Acts 20:32 NLT

Moving from Hurt to Hope

Trust God
Obey God
Love God
Forgive
Love your neighbor
Move on
Have faith
Hope in God
Seek God's will
Pray
Be wise
Wait—then run!

Endnotes

1   Kim Boyce, vocal recording of "Not Too Far from Here," by Ty Lacy and Steve Siler, released October 25, 1994, on *By Faith*, compact disc. Copyright © 1994 Ariose Music (ASCAP) (adm. at CapitolCMGPublishing.com) All rights reserved. Used by permission.

2   Kenneth Boa, *Conformed to His Image* (Grand Rapids, MI: Zondervan, 2001), 63.

3   "Trust and Obey," by John H. Sammis, 1887. Public domain.

4   John MacArthur and Wayne Mack, *Counseling: How to Counsel Biblically* (Nashville: Thomas Nelson, 2005), 55–56.

5   A.W. Tozer, *The Knowledge of the Holy* (San Francisco: Harper & Row, 1961), 1.

6   MacArthur and Mack, *Counseling: How to Counsel Biblically*, 153.

7   *The Answer: Authentic Faith for an Uncertain World (The Holy Bible New Century Version)* (Nashville: Thomas Nelson, 2003), 744.

8   John Baillie, *A Diary of Private Prayer* (New York: Fireside/Simon & Schuster, 1996), 45.

9   James Efird, *Biblical Books of Wisdom: A Study of Proverbs, Job, Ecclesiastes, and other Wisdom Literature in the Bible* (Eugene: Wipf and Stock Publishers, 1983), 62.

10 Stormie Omartian, *The Power of a Praying Woman* (Eugene, OR: Harvest House, 2002), 92.

11 J.I. Packer, *Knowing God* (Downer's Grove, IL: InterVarsity Press, 1993), 116.

12 Jay Adams, *The Christian Counselor's Manual: The Practice of Nouthetic Counseling* (Grand Rapids: Zondervan, 1973), 177.

13 Packer, *Knowing God*, 42.

14 W.E. Vine, Merrill F. Unger, and William White, Jr., *Vine's Expository Dictionary of Biblical Words* (Nashville: Thomas Nelson, 1985), 382.

15 Ibid., 297.

16 See "Strong's Greek: 5590," *Bible Hub*, accessed September 19, 2014, http://biblehub.com/greek/5590.htm

17 F.F. Bruce, *The International Bible Commentary* (Grand Rapids: M. Pickering/Zondervan, 1986), 1174.

18 *Vine's*, 603,2.

19 Efird, *Biblical Books of Wisdom*, 49.

20 *Devotional Classics: Selected Readings for Individuals and Groups*, eds. Richard J. Foster and James Bryan Smith (San Francisco: HarperOne, 2005), 51.

21 Baillie, *A Diary of Private Prayer*, 89.

22 Jared Pingleton, "The Role and Function of Forgiveness in the Psychotherapeutic Process," *Journal of Psychology and Theology* 17, no. 1 (1989): 27–35.

23 Jared Pingleton, "Why We Don't Forgive: A Biblical and Object Relations Theoretical Model for Understanding Failure in the Forgiveness Process," *Journal of Psychology and Theology* 25, no. 4 (1997): 403–13.

24 Darrell Puls, *The Road Home: A Guided Journey to Church Forgiveness and Reconciliation* (Eugene: Cascade Books, 2013), Kindle edition.

25 Lewis Smedes, "The Art of Forgiveness," *The Highland Shepherd*, accessed September 18, 2014, http://www.msgr.ca/msgr/Art%20of%20Forgiveness%20-%2005.pdf.

26 R.T. Kendall, "Forgiving the Unrepentant," *Christianity Today*, March 9, 2005, http://www.christianitytoday.com/ct/2005/march/29.78.html.

27 Smedes, "The Art of Forgiveness."

28 Ibid.

29 Lance Morrow, "Pope John Paul II Forgives His Would-Be Assassin," *Time*, January 19, 1984, http://content.time.com/time/magazine/article/0,9171,952295,00.html.

30 Jim Bakker, *I Was Wrong: The Untold Story of the Shocking Journey from PTL Power to Prison and Beyond* (Nashville: Thomas Nelson, 1997), 347.

31 Ibid., 31.

32 Puls, *The Road Home*.

33 Omartian, *The Power of a Praying Woman*, 51.

34 *The Answer: Authentic Faith for an Uncertain World*, 358.

35 Charles Stanley, "Ask Dr. Stanley: How can I love my enemies?" *In Touch Ministries*, accessed September 18, 2014, http://www.intouch.org/magazine/content/topic/ask_dr_stanley_february_2013#.U8ArQahQCkk.

36 Ron Steele, *Plundering Hell to Populate Heaven: Reinhard Bonnke's Vision* (Tulsa: Albury Press, 1990), 40.

37 Charles Stanley, "Ask Dr. Stanley."

38 Puls, *The Road Home*.

39 *Ever After: A Cinderella Story*, screenplay by Susannah Grant, Andy Tennant, and Rick Parks, Flower Films, 1998.

40 Baillie, *A Diary of Private Prayer*, 49, 121.

41 Omartian, *The Power of a Praying Woman*, 247.

42 Mark Batterson, *The Circle Maker: Praying Circles Around Your Biggest Dreams and Greatest Fears* (Grand Rapids: Zondervan, 2011), 132.

43 Kim Boyce, vocal recording of "Faith," by Denny Correll and Rhett Lawrence (Upper Lake Music/Rhettrhyme Music/ASCAP), released June 27,1989, on *Love Is You to Me*, Myrrh, 1989, compact disc. Copyright 1989 Rhettrhyme Music (Admin. by Brentwood-Benson Music Publishing, Inc.).

44 *The Woman's Study Bible* (Nashville: Thomas Nelson, 1995), 2046.

45 Ibid, 2104.

46 Steele, *Plundering Hell to Populate Heaven*, 26.

47 *The Answer: Authentic Faith for an Uncertain World*, 399.

48 Steele, *Plundering Hell to Populate Heaven*, 99.

49 Baillie, *A Diary of Private Prayer*, 113.

50 http://www.biblestudytools.com/commentaries/matthew-henry-concise/hebrews/6.html for *Matthew Henry's Concise Commentary* on Hebrew 6:19.

51 *Devotional Classics: Selected Readings for Individuals and Groups*, 39.

52 Packer, *Knowing God*, 23.

53 From a presentation at the Christian Ministries Church, Hot Springs, AR, Women's Conference, March 2014.

54 Barbara Hughes, *The Disciplines of a Godly Woman* (Wheaton, IL: Crossway Books, 2001), 41.

55 Richard J. Foster, *Celebration of Discipline*: *The Path to Spiritual Growth* (San Francisco: HarperSanFrancisco, 1978), 33,

56 *The Woman's Study Bible*, 1966.

57 Hannah Whitall Smith, *The Christian's Secret of a Happy Life* (as published by Christian Witness Co., now in public domain in the USA), www.ccel.org/ccel/smith_hw/secret.i.html, accessed Oct. 14, 2014.

58 Batterson, *The Circle Maker*, 72.

59 Baillie, *A Diary of Private Prayer*, 41.

60 Richard Blackaby, *Experiencing God* (Nashville: B & H Books, 2008), 37.

61 *Devotional Classics: Selected Readings for Individuals and Groups*, 98.

62 Brother Lawrence, *The Practice of the Presence of God* (Orlando, FL: Bridge Logos, 1999), 2.

63 Ibid.

64 *Frank Laubach, Letters by a Modern Mystic,(Colorado Springs: Purposeful Design Publications, 2007), 6 /22/1930*

65 *Devotional Classics: Selected Readings for Individuals and Groups*, 87-91.

66 Wesley Duewel, *Mighty Prevailing Prayer* (Grand Rapids: Zondervan, 1990), 11.

67 Ibid, 15.

68 Foster, *Celebration of Discipline*, 33.

69 Dietrich Bonhoeffer, *The Cost of Discipleship* (New York: Touchstone/Simon and Schuster, 1995), 166.

70 Omartian, *The Power of a Praying Woman*, 169.

71 Kim Boyce Koreiba, *There is a God*, 2011.

72 Packer, *Knowing God*, 80.

73 Finis Jennings Dake, *Dake Annotated Reference Bible* (Lawrenceville, GA: Dake Bible Sales, 2013), New Testament, 164, h.

74 Ibid.

75 Batterson, *The Circle Maker*, 164.